E.P. THOMPSON
COLLECTED POEMS

EDWARD THOMPSON

(PHOTO: BERROWS NEWSPAPERS)

E.P. THOMPSON

Collected Poems

EDITED BY FRED INGLIS

BLOODAXE BOOKS

ISBN: 1 85224 422 4

First published 1999 by
Bloodaxe Books Ltd,
P.O. Box 1SN,
Newcastle upon Tyne NE99 1SN.

Bloodaxe Books Ltd acknowledges
the financial assistance of Northern Arts.

Cover printing by J. Thomson Colour Printers Ltd, Glasgow.

Printed in Great Britain by
Cromwell Press Ltd, Trowbridge, Wiltshire.

Contents

Powers and Names 1986

INTRODUCTION: TRIBUTE AND MEMOIR

Edward Palmer Thompson, who died at the age of 69 in 1993, was one of the greatest English writers since the Second World War. Indeed, it would be to pay him the tribute he would most have relished himself to say that he was far and away the greatest writer to take as his mighty theme the Cold War which followed the more slaughterous one of 1939-45 and was presumably so-called because it killed a mere 17 million men, women and children, most of those from countries unfortunate enough to play no part in the world-historical process and in any case populated by people of alien tongues and curious skin colour.

Thompson is *the* writer of the Cold War. His prodigious, often single-handed efforts to oppose it with his typewriter, his amazing good looks and his gangling body, all allied to the passion of the word, probably broke his health. His fatal illness began in the autumn of 1989, after the Berlin Wall was pierced and the body of Imre Nagy, exhumed from the execution yard, was driven through the streets of Budapest to a decent grave, watched by his daughter and the silent multitudes of the city.

The range and prodigality of Thompson's writing over the 44 year span of the epoch is well known but unacknowledged *for itself.* This is hardly surprising when one remembers – can anybody already have forgotten? – the polemical occasion for so much of it. There are still volumes of his uncollected journalism to come and those volumes we have – *Writing by Candlelight, The Heavy Dancers* and *Double Exposure* – are offensive actions, guerrilla raids, sniping patrols, calls to street insurrection which duly received the official hostilities in reply.

I say 'journalism' but the term is almost as inclusive and con-tested as 'literature'. Thompson's journalism was a kind of scholarly 'folk-speaking' (the phrase is John Arlott's, another poet, public speaker and folk-hero; another good man, too). That is to say, it was addressed, as he once grandly put it in a famous pamphlet, 'to the people of England', and he remains a rare and, as I would want to add, exemplary case of a writer whose appeal to Englishness has something alive and good and strong in it which might still serve the English well at a time of the breaking of nations.

He once spoke movingly – a comradely letter, deliberately pub-lic, to a Marxist-Catholic Pole[1] – of his own literary provenance in this context. The classic text on freedom was for him Milton's

Areopagitica; the man from whom to learn angry, Irish and sardonic sarcasm in the face of the bland, concealed cruelties of power, Jonathan Swift; talk to Thompson of expropriation and the devastated peasantry 'and I am back with Wordsworth's Solitary', while the junior muse *Theoria* reappeared dressed in the remoralised Marxism of William Morris. Above all, it may be, he venerated William Blake: Blake for his extraordinary capacity to visualise the monster tendencies of the historical moment as vast and solid creatures of the imagination, moving with slow, dreadful actuality through the nightmare scenes of the *Prophetic Books*, Dante crossed with Gillray. But Blake also was his master for his reanimation of the rhythms of the King James Bible, for the way in which its noble Jacobean cadence and image was kept up by Leveller, Ranter and Muggletonian, its muscularity and force transmitted clear across two hundred years, never softened and pietised by the snowy-banded clerics in the pay of Old Corruption.

Blake was the subject of the last book Thompson finished,[2] and the Blake he fashions there is a man through whom an elaborate and complex formation may be said to speak, but whose voice is still distinctively his own for all that. Like Shakespeare, Blake utters so many voices not his own. Blake's formation is a rich compound of, firstly, the world and words of skilled, highly literate artisanal printers; secondly, the vigorous, argumentative and theologically racy market-place of the non-conformist sects and churches of the day, often driven underground for their inexcusable determination to press the precepts of the Bible home to the practice of politics; finally, the new, thrilling and garbled play of democratic ideas, a play which had its macabre melodrama acted out in the *Place de la Guillotine*, but which for Blake and his fellows brought a new purpose to a politics sundered by the venality and brutality of Whigs and Tories alike. For them as for Thompson, politics and history, between which, as Eric Hobsbawm claimed,[3] he made little distinction, were the study of how the world is *and* how it ought to be.

Blake's moment was of course the moment of *The Making of the English Working Class*.[4] This astonishing work is, you might say, Thompson's version of a Prophetic Book. It is a work of scholarly history; it is a vast Romantic-Marxist novel. Record and archive and citation are faithfully observed; the heroes and heroines of working-class formation, Somerville, Bamford, Joanna Southcott, speak as they speak in the original texts, but all are gathered into a collective making of membership, a coming-to-creative-consciousness which is their grand and contradictory confection of culture, defined by Thompson as 'handled experience' and 'way of struggle'.[5]

Thompson's history-writing, like Blake's prophesying, is intent on telling a true story about the past which is also a way of illuminating the present. And like Blake, like all great poets, he was at pains to refuse simple bromides, of either a theoretic or a party-political kind. His study of the Black Act of the mid-eighteenth century, whereby freeborn Englishmen hunting their supper were turned into poachers and menaced, in some cases, by execution, names for what they were the graspingness of the owners of Windsor Forest and the toadying obedience of the judge.[6] At the same time, Thompson finds in the staid transcripts not only the honest fight of the oppressed, allegiance to whom was his first historical principle as well as his method, but also a light shining from the blind justice of the day and still burning through the rigged evidence and fixed witnesses of the courts.

His writings on the little matter of English justice are more than strictly historical. In a splendidly comic as well as faithful passage of parody, he once caught near perfectly the prose of an Elizabethan gentleman, plausibly helped out by a bracing thimbleful of anachronism, writing of his sudden outrage when the government of the day was judged by him, in Thompson's own, immortal pun on Mrs Thatcher's easy and confident way with things, 'to be taking liberties that were once ours'. As Squire Edwd Tomson, he wrote:

> At my Gate I was accosted by Master Giles, Wheelwright of Powicke, he that is said to be of a new Puritan persuason & to be a great Reader by Candlelight & to have strange Lecturers to visitt at his House. He greeted me uncouthly & wthout doffing his Hatt & he said that the State ran in Ill Courses & that the Queen had bad Advisors & that he and some mean Fellows do intend to gett up a Remonstrance to the Comons House willing em to pass an Act of Attaynder of the Queens Privy Council & her chief Secretarys of State. And further he blurted out that as he had alwayes held me to be an Honest Country Gentleman (thow no great Thinker he was pleased to add) he had come to Sollicit my Hand in this Affair.

> I raised myself High in my Saddle, the better to bring down my Whipp upon his Back. But as I turned I saw on every Side the noble Trees planted by my Forefathers Cutt down & Burned & Natures Poison all at Waste, & it came to Mind how the Dealers & the sly Agents of Forrayn Lands & the Privy Contrivers of Silly Peevish Cheeting Tryals of State do bring our Country into Contempt, do lead our Queen into foul & false Courses, & do blight the Labour & the Honour of Men of every Degree.

> Come into my Study, Goodman Giles, said I. I will take Counsel with thee. And I do assure thee, I keepe no Mirrours in Episcopi Hall.[7]

11

There is a mastery of idiom here which is beyond a joke. It is apparent in several of the poems which follow, notably the 'Scenario for the Flight into Egypt' as well as in *Power and Names*.

In 'Scenario' the film-producer jots down his list of imagery –

> Blow up a woman's grieving face?
> Blow up a bloody dog? –
>
> ...The rest is trite...
> Let's see... Di da di da...
> Bundles and broken carts. Roads machine-gunned.
> Trucks overturned and burning.
> Swarms of white-faced kids. Detritus of several cities –
> The usual parts. Expensive all those extras...

The callousness is played off against the piteousness of things. The producer makes the spectacle for those who do not live and feel the horrors on the spot. They will feel *something*; and then, since they are not the ones dead, turn to their affairs, or to the latest news. The producer feels nothing for the subjects, only for the objects in his story. He is, of course, horrible (the 'bloody dog' is also a bloody dog; sure, he uses real blood, what do you take him for?), but not only horrible. Somebody has to show us these things, haven't they? Thompson turns on him savagely – savage meiosis and the bitter gall of sarcasm are two of his most characteristic tropes. He gives him the words of a compassionate man, pausing as he looks at the loved, familiar scene. Then he snatches them back.

> I see them resting at a turning in the road,
> Where Joseph scoops a hollow in the sand,
> And Mary gently lowers her heavy load.
>
> Cut. Egypt. Zoom in on a squat...

The quiet pentameters speak themselves, not in the producer's voice; the long-loved names, Joseph, Mary, the child, gather the shadows of old poems and paintings above them. Then, 'Cut'.

The great contribution of socialism to Western thought is its strong sympathy for and identification with history's losers. In the *Fall of Hyperion*, Keats, another of Thompson's poets (as you'd expect) writes of the visionary goddess Moneta, visited by the poet who must mediate that vision. She tells him:

> 'None can usurp this height,' returned that shade,
> 'But those to whom the miseries of the world
> Are misery, and will not let them rest.'

Such was Thompson; but the way the miseries pressed upon his senses did not make him miserable. It made him, Perry Anderson once wrote, 'our finest socialist writer today', by turns 'passionate and playful, caustic and delicate, colloquial and decorous, [without] peer on the Left'.[8] Misery: the hideous, avoidable misery of the wretched of the earth, and the cruel indifference of power and system, whether of a Stalinist, a Maoist or a liberal capitalist provenance did not make Thompson miserable; these things made him angry, angry with the bitter humour taught him, I would guess, by the army, but angry also in the way a generous-hearted man is angry at *avoidable* suffering and horror. Such anger is of the kind which dissolves easily into spontaneous joy and open geniality when things are put right.

As they *can* be put right. Socialism is, in spite of this now dying and abominable century, above all a doctrine of hope, and the hope is for justice and mercy. Socialism's two great origins, Marxism and Christianity (and, pledged to neither, both moved in Thompson's bones and blood) taught alike that those two mighty values are our only hope, and this hope was stiffened in him by the lessons he found in history that his own country had played a part in the historical formation of a sufficiently human theory of justice. The 'freeborn Englishman' was more than a fiction, in spite of all that this or that gouty old bully of a hanging judge had done to put him down. The possibility of justice and the vile comicality of what power does to it are the themes of his poetry, as of his history; as of all his writing.

Unlike comrade-socialists of a more theoretic bent, let alone those on a world scale who found themselves with power in their hands and could afford to postpone any rendezvous with either justice or mercy until a lot of more practical scores had been settled in the usual ways, Thompson was at once a patriot as well as that hardly compatible figure, someone who believed in the necessity of love.

There is little demand for patriotism amongst high-minded Leftists at the present, but then love does not much appear in their indexes either. Both words belong happily enough, however, in the works and lives of those great writers amongst whom Thompson moved so easily in his imagination, spirit and memory – Blake, Wordsworth, Yeats, T.S. Eliot, Ted Hughes; Morris, Ruskin, Tom Paine.

Those Englishmen, come to that, that Irishman and that American, were patriotic in the sense that the rhythms of their life and the rhythms of the literature they loved were mutually embedded: phrases and cadences swam up out of the past and into their lives *naturally*. Patriotism was then a more or less metaphysical matter.

It certainly wasn't a matter of supposing that what one's country did must be well done. Thompson was an unremitting enemy of imperialism, like his father; he was an internationalist, a *European* socialist, like his brother. But he once addressed a younger generation than his with this reproach, blasted out of him by his vivid sense that, in *his* youth, *his* country had fashioned this unprecedented kind of army in order to oppose the most cruel and hideous enemy the world had ever seen. It fashioned that army at a time when it was far from clear that that enemy *could* be defeated; but it had to be fought because, well, it was so frightful that a young man or woman could hardly live with themselves if each had not, in the affecting little understatement of the day, 'done their bit'.

> I recall a resolute and ingenious civilian army, increasingly hostile to the conventional military virtues, which became – far more than any of my younger friends will begin to credit – an anti-fascist and consciously anti-imperialist army. Its members voted Labour in 1945: knowing why, as did the civilian workers at home. Many were infused with socialist ideas and expectations wildly in advance of the tepid rhetoric of today's Labour leaders...
>
> It is difficult to explain how memories affect one in middle life. For months, the past stretches behind one, as an inert record of events. Then, without forewarning, the past seems suddenly to open itself up inside one – with a more palpable emotional force than the vague present – in the gesture of a long-dead friend, or in the recall of some 'spot of time' imbued with incommunicable significance. One is astonished to find oneself, while working in the garden or pottering about the kitchen, with tears on one's cheeks.
>
> I have found myself like this more than once since reading Mr Pincher's book. I have no notion what the tears are about. They are certainly not those of self-pity. There may be something in them of shame, that we should have let that world be degraded into this. There is also fury – that younger people, and among these some whom I most approve or admire, should have had this foul historical con passed upon them – should suppose that this is all that that generation was... Pincher's sort of people!
>
> I can now see what was wrong with that generation. It was too bloody innocent by half, and some of them were too open to the world, and too loyal to each other to live.[9]

That unaffected, raw protestation is hardly artful writing; but it is absolutely continuous with his more wrought and majestic effects, even when – above all when – he is taunting his own inefficacy and, in doing so, affirming an older belief that after all, the poet's words and the historian's hunt together on behalf of the human. Against the armies of the night, they guard the victory hidden in defeat.

Oh, royal me! Unpoliced imperial man
And monarch of my incapacity

To aid my helpless comrades as they fall –
Lumumba, Nagy, Allende: alphabet
Apt to our age! In answer to your call

I rush out in this rattling harvester
And thrash you into type. But what I write
Brings down no armoured bans, no Ministers

Of the Interior interrogate.
No one bothers to break in and seize
My verses for subversion of the State:

Even the little dogmas do not bark.
I leave my desk and peer into the world.
Outside the owls are hunting. Dark

Has harvested the moon. Imperial eyes
Quarter the ground for fellow creaturehood:
Small as the hour some hunted terror cries.

I go back to my desk...

Reading this, I think of those wonderful remarks of F.R. Leavis (of whom Thompson once said 'that it would be good to have fought some of *his* battles alongside him') when, writing of Thomas Hardy's 'After a Journey', he praises the poet's *sincerity*, which is to say the genius with which the poet *realises*, that is, makes real and immediate to the readers, the actuality of the experience, thinking in it and with it, with an absolute fidelity both to its truthfulness and the significance the experience has for him. And Leavis goes on,

> It is a case in which we know from the art what the man was like; we can be sure, that is, what personal qualities we should have found to admire in Hardy if we could have known him.[10]

Leavis has been reproached for something artless and old-fashioned in his criterion of sincerity and it may by now be so. If it is, so much the worse for poetry.

Even at our present, postmodern moment, for a poet to put such a sincerity at the centre of artistic things is to chime strongly with all common and uncommon readers. For a man and a writer like Thompson it would have been unthinkable not to do so. His was a natural and ordinary allegiance to a sane, affirmative, noble and egalitarian idiom of politics and poetry alike, and it was the point of his history and his ethics to appeal to that same allegiance in the hearts of all those who might be counted comrades, and for whom literature means what it says, simply, sensuously, passionately.

Not that Thompson cannot pick up and drop a poetic persona with the best of them. But in 'My Study' he writes as himself, sitting in his plain, bare-boarded study overlooking quiet meadows above Worcester, harvesting and gathering the pain-filled words, propping a few small jokes against the facts of betrayal and execution, walking at the end off the great stage of history into a dark night in the small, safe hours.

This is a man and a writer determined to live in the eye of his historical times and, like Yeats, to spit into it for all it has done to transfigure his history. Living in your times is an exigent vocation; it means you can mark no distance between your work and your life. This is not to foist upon Thompson any piety to the effect that the personal is the political. If that is so, something has gone badly wrong and we cannot see how to keep reasons of state out of the everyday costs of loving. The killing tedium of politics would then swamp the lives we want to lead, and fill with their blankness the livelihood we confect for ourselves. But as Thompson himself said of the continued duty to oppose the 'exterminism' of nuclear weaponry, 'it would ill become us not to play out our old roles to the end'. The political duty, like the aesthetic effect, is to affirm value against power. Too much value, as you might say, and poetry turns sentimental; too much power, and realism turns to ruthlessness.

All this is less a matter of balance (as they say) and much more a commitment to be faithful to the recalcitrance of the historical facts of life so far as they are determinable. It is not a bad maxim for a poet and, as we have seen, Thompson deliberately ignored, insofar as one man may ever do so, the deep and high divisions of labour which mark out the ground of intellectual industry in our time. Poetry, journalism, memoirs, analysis of the politics of Cold War for a dozen different audiences, platform rhetoric, scholarly but resolutely unacademic history, his one long and unclassifiable novel *The Sykaos Papers*,[11] literary criticism, his mighty biography of William Morris (the first to take the measure of that great man's political stamina, the first also to treat carefully Morris's translations of the Icelandic sagas), Thompson worked without self-deprecation and as he needed them in all these genres.

His poetics, therefore, suffuses all his work. Like any serious style of writing, his was both personal and impersonal and, either way, hard-won by the handling of hard old experience, the gift of happiness and the irruptions of tragedy.

He had daunting examples to follow and was, at times, daunted by them. His father, also Edward, was a successful novelist and

16

poet, a Methodist preacher who taught Indian history at Oxford and lived Indian history in India; an associate of Gandhi and a close friend of Nehru, rewarded, like his son, by British secret surveillance. A tireless and public advocate of Indian independence, husband of a no-less-independent American wife, Thompson's father was a compelling example of a forgotten hero in the history of Empire: the brave and cultivated scholar-dissenter without whose principled opposition and active example the end of that Empire might have been far bloodier and less creditable than it was. The figure of descent is clear.

The second example was his brother Frank, born in 1920, four years earlier than Edward, executed by Bulgarian Fascists in the hills above Sofia at the age of 24, forever caught at that age, still Edward Thompson's senior when Edward Thompson was more than twice his age.[12]

Frank was a fearsome figure to have as an elder brother. He was an astonishing linguist, learning Latin and Greek, French and German at Winchester (to which he won a scholarship) before teaching himself another half-dozen languages including Italian, Polish, Serbian, Bulgarian and Russian while listening to the radio it was his military duty to monitor while on active service in the Western desert.

He had been to Oxford for a year mastering the classical literature his brother always regretted not knowing, been undergraduate sweethearts with the novelist Iris Murdoch, become one of those admirably high-minded, idealistic English communists who saw plainly the hideous lineaments of a world-threatening Fascism, and against his parents' wishes volunteered at 20 to go to war.

He volunteered again, after attending the invasion of Sicily, to be parachuted behind the lines as a liaison officer attached to Special Operations Executive in order to link up first with Yugoslav then with Bulgarian partisans. After desperate endeavours on the run from the Fascists, starving, drenched and chilled to the bone by mountain sleet, his British comrades dead and his Bulgarians hopelessly ill-equipped, he was captured, subjected to a rigged trial, and shot together with the captured partisans. Years later, his younger brother speculated bitterly that the British authorities may have been complicit in the execution. 'Somebody winked,' he wrote; and 'There is clear evidence, even in those portions of the British records which have been released, of very heavy and specific weeding between March and June 1944.'[13]

Edward followed his brother into the army, commanding at the age of 20 a troop of tanks through the Italian campaign from Cassino to Perugia and northwards. He too was a communist; his 'Song for 1945' in this collection came out in the left-wing weekly *Our Time* in February of that year. He went out to Tito's new and heretical communist state, Yugoslavia, to help build the state railway alongside Dorothy his wife-to-be, fellow-socialist, fellow-historian, and came home to join those like-minded spirits, shaped by the democratic hopes and victories of a dreadful war, who staffed the incipiently open university configured in university departments of extra-mural studies.[14] The students were working people, men and women of small means with little but their strong respect for learning and a craving for culture on damp evenings in chilly halls to keep them on the course. But they came to ask questions about experience which officially educated knowledge had never raised, and discovered from Edward Thompson, then living in a large, cold, hospitable, grit-stone house in the dark town of Halifax, that their forebears, the weavers, spinners, saggers, dyers, printers, Chartists and Methodists of south Yorkshire and Lancashire had made history by making themselves a social class.

The rest of Thompson's heroic tale is itself history. Invited to start a centre for labour history at Warwick soon after the new university's inception, he changed its remit to the Centre for Social History, but resigned a few years later in 1972 to become a freelance writer, with the support of his wife and her academic salary. The Thompsons moved to a sometime diocesan mansion with a splendid portico outside Worcester. Edward became the kind of old-fashioned, English radical-of-letters whose demise has been so very exaggerated for so long. The influence of the polemical pamphlet, of no fixed address and without a system of distribution, had been dismissed by commentators years ago but Thompson's unforgettable malediction *Protest and Survive*,[15] spoken over the agreement to install US cruise missiles on Greenham Common and at Molesworth, sold well over 100,000 copies long before going into a Penguin edition (all royalties to the movement).

It was, in effect, the rallying call which shaped and focused that vague, pervasive resentment and that wholly justified fearfulness in Britain, North America, Holland, Italy, Germany, at the brutal and extravagant dangerousness of playing for political advantage with world incineration. *Protest and Survive* was the first loud and coherent declaration that the structure of feeling which had contained the Cold War had split open and was pouring away in a new tide. Ronald Reagan and Mrs Thatcher couldn't see it; Mikhail Gorbachev could. A decade later, the crowds in the streets and squares of Gdansk, Leipzig, Berlin, Budapest, Prague and Timisoara finished things off. Thompson was not only proved right, his words in his style had been a prime saboteur of iron curtain and Berlin Wall.

I cannot doubt that the colossal self-sacrifice and overwork of the years from 1979 to his premature death wounded him in body and spirit. Already well known as a travelling intellectual in the great tradition of William Morris and Jean-Paul Sartre, he became a celebrity of the quite new kind which late capitalist communications have devised on behalf of the competition of ideas.

The adulation and vilification which follow such promotion exact a hidden toll. By nature passionate, impulsive and touchy, Edward Thompson responded warmly but warily to the fame which his sense of public duty brought him. Being human, he loved it; being a fine and a fond as well as a visionary man, he also deplored it.

Either way, the spurs of fame never scratched his style or signature. He remained always a *public* writer. The poetry sorts with that. At the same time, a public writer in private Old England must be a queer creature. He or she must compound a poetry of many voices as well as one distinctive voice.

Thompson named his pieties, as we know. Milton, Swift, Blake and Wordsworth are his literary masters; just as audibly, so too are Yeats and Auden. There is a quatrain by Yeats which Thompson often quoted – he knew, of course, great tracts of his best-loved poems by heart – and its characteristic mixture of domestic imagery with grandly political and mythical resonance, such as Yeats himself found in Blake, is what Thompson looked for in prose and poetry and life itself.

> What if the Church and State
> Are the mob that howls at the door?
> Wine shall run thick to the end,
> Bread taste sour.

Auden, too, ran through his head and tripped off his tongue, that laconic, clipped way Auden had of prefiguring a whole action, shadowy but momentous in context, plain as day to see, bitterly funny to hear, ripples in Thompson's feeling and the style he made to express it. In his lectures about his brother and the doomed campaign in Bulgaria, he quotes 'Missing', leaving the lines at the right moment.

> The tall, unwounded leader
> Of doomed companions, all
> Whose voices in the rocks
> Are now perpetual.
> Fighters for no one's sake
> Who died beyond the border...

19

Thompson fashioned his style out of the immense and punishing plenitude of his own temperament and his historical experience: father, brother,[16] War and Party; wife, children, house and historiography; teaching history to a handful of woollen workers, preaching peace to sixty thousand people in Trafalgar Square, standing outside Wick Episcopi late at night looking up at Orion's sword, Sirius the Dog, and the unsleeping nuclear bombers flying below them.

So the poems came in between the endless demands for papers or reviews, the crying need to address the next crisis in the columns of the *Guardian*, the *Nation, New Society, Peace News*, the continuing labours of scholarship. It is the same voice, no matter what the form, and being an Englishman speaking in public, intimacy touches his manner, there is a glimpse of the private between the bars of the public, the touching tenderness of 'Lullaby' – not many poetic Englishmen have played the nursing mother in print – is matched in public by the hard control and bitter hatred of 'In Praise of Hangmen', written just after the hangman's field-day in Hungary in 1956.

Tenderness, sardonic anger; rage and hatred; the bitingly accurate comicality of the film producer in 'Scenario for the Flight into Egypt', the bitter jokes – 'A cartload of salted fish was hitched to its litter' (the detail comes from the records) – the violent compression of a tradition of thought (murderous thought, as it happens), as in 'History Lessons'; the breadth of political vision; it is a lot for an occasional poet to encompass. The poems show signs of this occasionality. The manner is at times stiff and unpractised, perhaps most noticeably in the most ambitious sequence *Power and Names*, with which the collection ends. It was prompted by a visit to China and to the amazing collection of the Emperor Quin Shi-huang's lifesize terracotta warriors unearthed from an underground cavern between 1974 and 1980, dated from the second century. It may put the literary historian in mind of Ezra Pound's and Arthur Waley's translations from the Chinese. It has its awkwardness, its at times too-insistent tone of scornfulness, its sardonic meioses. But I cannot think of a political poem to match it for epic grandeur and grand wit since before the death of Robert Lowell.

Michael Schmidt wrote:

> What particularly strikes me is the way in which Thompson uses, even in his more quiet poems, a very public rhetoric, speaking as though Milton could still live and apparently, for the most part, un-deflected by the poetic revolutions of the first part of this century. I at once admire and am to some extent chilled by the assurance of the poems, so strange at this time of day and, for me, in the end, so curiously partial in relation to the experiences they directly or obliquely allude to.[17]

20

One sees what he means. Thompson writes as though, in Keats's image, 'the cliff of poetry does [*not*] tower over him'. Ben Thompson, his son (also a poet like his sister Kate), has told me of his father's admiration for Ted Hughes, as well as of his simple sense of his equality with other writers, admiring them for sure – jealous it may be of their greater gifts – but calmly writing as one of them, moving unabashed and as a familiar through the crowded rooms of the mansions of poetry.

In a striking letter, Thompson once wrote to a friend [18] about his response to John Berryman's *36 Sonnets,* which he had been reading for the first time. His criticism is extremely searching, too much so almost, for it is clear from what he says that poetry is for him, as it is in all Romantic aesthetics, the ultimate technique for telling truths about the soul in all its nakedness. The risks involved in this quest are of course immense, and those who have come of recent years to scoff at such a view of poetry are likely to be those whose souls have not much in them of truth or anything else. But Thompson's remarks bear out, it may be, the applicability of Leavis's criterion of 'sincerity' as a test of that poetry in which what it is to be sincere is indeed to think in and with the actuality of experience, and so to render it on the page that the reader may realise the poet's purposes by way of a different, sympathetic response.

Thompson wrote:

> They include some of the best poems I have read in a long time... Perhaps half of them are very good indeed: I don't always understand the other half, and it is not just the privacy and symbolism but also a way Berriman [*sic*] sometimes has of ducking his own emotions and conclusions in preference to anything that could be accused of sentimentalism. There is at many points a fear of that: and one understands and goes with it, because it is out of that resistance that some of the truth and realisation comes. And yet some of the poems which I now think the best are ones in which he allows the feeling to run through even if it borders on sentiment. In others there is something of that remote, obsessional, self-enclosed, self-agitating, self-destroying emotion which is a true part of experience, truthfully and remarkably conveyed, and yet at the same time not something 'I like', something I know too well and sense too closely at my side to 'like'. And there are other kinds of feeling in them too close to be read without pain... I shall certainly return to these poems: and they are certainly the sort of poem that makes one want to try also, show one a new way of writing, a way one might follow but with one's own accent and voice.

I have grouped the poems in a rough chronology. But Thompson himself rearranged them several times, so the details of his development are not always clear. The sequence *Infant and Emperor,* for example, although sent out to his friends instead of a Christmas card in 1983, included some poems written 20 or more years before, and others written to the moment. Thompson wove them into a little seasonal posy and had them printed by his faithful comrade Martin Eve at Merlin Press for despatch in the most menacing weather of late Cold War. 'A Place called Choice' was written in Halifax across several months of 1950 and, you could say, puts one much in mind of the poetry of Thompson's great friend, the American poet Thomas McGrath, himself the subject of a lengthy literary-critical eulogy by Thompson.[19]

McGrath's poetry has the same sweeping self-confidence as Thompson's, a simplicity and ruggedness one might think of as typically American, remembering at the same time that Thompson's mother was American. McGrath also writes as though the modern movement had never happened, speaks innocently as a man speaking to men without reckoning up or alluding to the echoes of other voices listeners might hear in his. He is, you might say, a Whitman for the Wobblies, but you must say so without the least trace of condescension. The titles of McGrath's best poems – 'Longshot O'Leary's Garland of Practical Poesie', 'Letter to an Imaginary Friend', 'Witness to the Times' – indicate his ambitions and, Ginsberg being dead, his sometime timeliness.

There's nothing much to be gained by speculating on McGrath's poetic influence on Thompson but his example fixes something of Thompson's own ambitions as well as offering a way to measure Thompson's heroic place in an unheroic present.

The present of course is always unheroic. Certain creatures put away such a man as Thompson when the Cold War ended, wars being the time for heroes and the war being over. But the unignorable force of these poems keeps breaking out; they come shouldering their way into the mild-mannered and inaudible conversation of poetry at the present time.

Schmidt's judgement catches their nature, in its way. This is indeed a man speaking to men and women in their real language, a man moreover of whom it is true that he is 'endued with a more lively sensibility... than is common' and that sensibility is equally compounded of the anger any generous-spirited person must feel at what states do with power, together with that happily truculent insubordination, that vivid tenderness of heart and quickness of human allegiance which were Thompson's very own. If the faults of the poetry include an over-generalised expression of human sympathy and a curmudgeonliness towards those particular admirers who for one reason or another offended him, then that too was part of the man.

The poet, the man, and the style are one. This collection bears witness to that claim. That is what in the older and better ethics to which Thompson gave his name is meant by integrity. Those ethics are at one with an aesthetics in which poetry is the best, because the sanest, plainest and most affirmative speech of a free citizen, speaking on behalf of his or her comrades.

Renewing the old speech in order to keep it speakable is the poet's task. For all the directness and cheerful freedoms of Edward Thompson's poetic manner, there are surely many echoes of T.S. Eliot in these pages. Unlike many on the Left with tin ears and concrete ideologies, Thompson the writer felt all through his being Eliot's passion for his sacred places – Little Gidding, the Dry Salvages – the absoluteness of his concern 'to purify the language of the tribe'. For him as, indeed, for Eliot, the language of history and the language of politics were one and the same. Over the years of Thompson's writing life the language of politics had been made filthy with dishonest use. The poems that follow do their bit towards cleaning up that horribly polluted environment.

FRED INGLIS

Notes

1. 'An Open Letter to Leszek Kolakowski', reprinted in E.P. Thompson, *The Poverty of Theory* (Merlin Press, 1978).

2. *Witness Against the Beast: William Blake and the Moral Law* (Cambridge University Press, 1993).

3. Eric Hobsbawm, 'Edward Palmer Thompson', *Proceedings of the British Academy*, 90 (1995), pp.521-39

4. First published by Victor Gollancz in 1963 when Thompson was 39; a revised edition with an extended reply to his critics appeared as Penguin number 1000, in the climacteric year of 1968.

5. In a celebrated review of Raymond Williams's 'The Long Revolution', *New Left Review*, nos 9, 10, 11 (1961-62).

6. *Whigs and Hunters: the origins of the Black Act* (Allen Lane, 1975).

7. *Writing by Candlelight* (Merlin Press, 1980), pp.96-7.

8. Perry Anderson, *Arguments within British Marxism* (Verso, 1980), p.1.

9. *Writing by Candlelight*, pp.131, 132-3.

10. F.R. Leavis, 'Reality and Sincerity', *A Selection from 'Scrutiny'*, edited by F.R. Leavis (Cambridge University Press, 1968), p.257.

11. In which he masters at one go the peculiar formalism of post-modernism: *The Sykaos Papers* (Pantheon and Bloomsbury, 1988).

12. As Thompson wrote in a short book edited by Dorothy Thompson, posthumously published as Edward Thompson, *Beyond the Frontier: The politics of a failed mission: Bulgaria 1944* (Merlin Press, 1997).

13. *Beyond the Frontier*, 97-98.

14. Their tale is excellently sketched out by John McIlroy in the introduction to *Border Country: Raymond Williams in Adult Education* (NIACE, 1993). See also Roger Fieldhouse, *Adult Education and the Cold War* (University of Leeds, 1985).

15. First published in 1979.

16. A selection of Frank's poems appears in the collection of his writings edited by Edward and his mother as *There is a Spirit in Europe* (Gollancz, 1947).

17. Letter to me, 18 August 1994.

18. Private correspondence not dated. Some time in 1975.

19. 'Homage to Thomas McGrath', in *The Heavy Dancers* (Merlin Press, 1985).

E.P THOMPSON: A SELECT BIBLIOGRAPHY

Books and collected essays

William Morris: Romantic to Revolutionary (London: Lawrence & Wishart, 1955; rev. edn, New York: Pantheon, 1977).

The Making of the English Working Class (London: Victor Gollancz, 1963; 2nd edn with a new postscript, Harmondsworth: Penguin, 1968; 3rd edn with a new preface, 1980).

Whigs and Hunters: The Origins of the Black Act (London: Allen Lane, 1975; reprinted with a new postscript, Harmondsworth: Penguin, 1977).

The Poverty of Theory and Other Essays (London: Merlin; New York: Monthly Review Press, 1978).

Writing by Candlight (London: Merlin, 1980).

Zero Option (London: Merlin, 1982; in USA, *Beyond the Cold War*, New York: Pantheon, 1982).

Double Exposure (London: Merlin, 1985).

The Heavy Dancers (London: Merlin, 1985; in USA: *The Heavy Dancers*, New York: Pantheon, 1985 – this edition incorporates *Double Exposure* but excludes selected essays of the British edition.

The Sykaos Papers (London: Bloomsbury; New York: Pantheon, 1988).

Customs in Common (New York & London: Viking, 1991).

Witness Against the Beast: William Blake and the Moral Law (Cambridge University Press, 1993; paperback, 1994; New York: New Press, 1993).

Alien Homage: Edward Thompson and Rabindranath Tagore (Bombay: Oxford University Press [India], 1993).

Persons and Polemics (London: Merlin, 1994 paperback only; in USA, *Making History*, New York: New Press, paperback and hardback.

Beyond the Frontier: The politics of a failed mission: Bulgaria 1944, edited by Dorothy Thompson (London: Merlin, 1997).

The Romantics (New York: New Press, 1997; London: Merlin, 1998).

Edited works

There is a Spirit in Europe: A Memoir of Frank Thompson, with T.J. Thompson (London: Victor Gollancz, 1947).

The Railway: An Adventure in Construction (London: The British-Yugoslav Association, 1948).

Out of Apathy (London: Stevens & Sons/New Left Books, 1960).

The May Day Manifesto, with Raymond Williams and Stuart Hall (published by subscription, 1967); rev. edn, edited by Raymond Williams (Harmondsworth: Penguin, 1968).

Warwick University Ltd (Harmondsworth: Penguin, 1973).

Albion's Fatal Tree, edited by D. Hay, P. Linebaugh, J.G. Rule, E.P. Thompson & C. Winslow (London: Allen Lane, 1975).

Protest and Survive, with Dan Smith (Harmondsworth: Penguin, 1980).

Exterminism and Cold War, edited by F. Halliday, R. Bahro & E.P. Thompson (London: Verso, 1982).

Mad Dogs: The U.S. Raids on Libya, edited by E.P. Thompson & Mary Kaldor (London: Pluto, 1986).

COLLECTED POEMS

EARLY POEMS

(1940–1947)

Redshank

Reeling from the reedbanks, you cry your outcast cry, like three curls
on a girl's forehead or a lonely spiral of peat smoke,
and beating fish-silver, flashing fins, you scatter tokens
like feathers of weather-worn wildernesses, the wide-wind skirl

and whirl of the plover, the wailing of waders on water-wastes
through dark, castaway dawns and lands like the ends of the world,
where the sea-sand wall welcomes no man. Warden
of the marshes they call you, and your call when you have ceased

waits in the air, – no warning, but an unanswered question, of lost
          lover
of war, and women weeping, and the wonder of wet valleys,
that wanders with geese, firm in formation, to the haunt of heron
and black-coated duck and brigand gull the whole world over.

This most in winter, when mud-flats form platforms for legs,
like pink pencils printing stars, or, later, feet hammer near nest;
but in summer, when life is no longer a question,
and the snipe spins a soft-sounding switchback over his eggs,

sailing along silent estuaries, you are seen among sedges,
the geese are forgotten, and grebes grace the shallow lakes,
and your call becomes confident, in down-drooping love-dance, –
          a token
with wings like ploughshares, of dash and freedom, of heights
          without hedges.

[1940, published in the Kingswood School magazine *Piazza*]

For a Friend of Childhood, Killed in the Air

You fell in a wild ladder of panic from the sky, and were dead.
And now you descend carelessly a ladder of years in my head,
and weary with the gravity of Time you fall beyond our reach;
your young yesterday falls away, drowned like a sailor in the blue
coral waters of the past, and we may only watch like a few
survivors in the wreck of the sea. There is nothing that speech
can do that will move you.

Like any eye of life you focused all near suns onto the stage
of your own consciousness; the lens fell with your flesh, the cage
of light was void, only a prologue played. And we will never learn
what leap and shout of sun, what shadows then were lost; this secret
fell with you. All I remember is your irrelevant and sacred
youth, the carol of your life, chorus of limbs. But now our lawns,
our lilac-land, mock at me, say they were only an ending.

O, you might have made a neat and brilliant tapestry of your lucky
life, but that your luck was built upon the curse of lackeys
and the vast commotions of wealth. With your neat hands you might
have built pavilions in a brilliant land of sun, had it been magic
waved you your fortune, not a whip of gold. But there was only logic
when your sun blinked once, invisible and excessively bright,
and went out.

For your childhood had plotted your death. You were born in a caul
of values not of your making; and above your web of sun the foul
and rotted pattern that had nourished a few thousand families
hooded your futile history. And while you ran along the rails
planted in gilt-edged lines before you, the future was on your trail
like a long lighted fuse under your singing life, and finally
it flushed the plot in flames, finished the pity of it all.

You are the first to leave the garden where we grew, and pass the
      sentry
into the huge hangars of death. You will never leave that country.
We may only run a pencil of sorrow through your damaged story.
Your guilt was the inheritance of luck. But time is short today
for poetry or parting. Your luck must be for all, or roundelays
like yours repeat, ending the tune in skulls. And I am only sorry
you will not see new teeth sprout in these gaping jaws.

[Andover, 1941, published in the Kingswood School magazine *Piazza*]

Timepiece

Old Father Time, my darling, sows; he does not reap, –
and from his sack of grain only a fingerful of seed
was spared for us. No, we've not had much time
together, dear, not the full bushel and load that lovers need.

This war we've been too busy, love, though certainly
what richness we have had would take a century to reap,
and you have left a quickness and a laugh in me,
and a great steadiness we found together as we fell asleep.

But Time is action, movement, Time is what we do,
and what we do is out of what old Time has done to us,
and there's no seed of time for us to grudge our loss
if fiercer knowing, larger love will follow what our fighting does.

Yet you'll forgive me if a passing sadness falls
like river mist; it is our place in history makes us this,
and I am glad of it; but if I'm ever back and if we meet
we'll gently touch each other, darling, we will very gently kiss,

and we will claim from Time a brimming thimble-weight,
and Time will stop for us, and history can wait.

[Written on the boat taking Thompson to active service
in north Africa, October 1943]

Untitled

I used to think I didn't like this country, – eucalyptus and cork
don't seem so friendly to an Englishman who's used to oak
and beech; and I'd not take a mile of sand for one good foot of chalk.
But all last night it rained, flooding my tent, and after all
dawn was a well-washed cyclamen in a land of waterfalls
and the brooks spoke the same language that the becks of England
       spoke.

And I thought I didn't like the people here, – brushwood and mud
will not keep out malaria nor even flies, and farming shifting sand
makes shiftless men, as does the stench of towns where dogs run mad.
But then today I saw the Arab boy patiently build his shed,
torn down by last night's rain; and, later, when the orange-seller made
a hard bargain with me, he smiled at me and also made a friend.

And I could see no promise in this country, but I've changed my mind;
I know they'll tell you rain and smiling aren't the stuff of politics,
and I'll agree, but such things answer me that even in this land
you'll not set back man's will to win, nothing will cancel out, not
       plague or sand
the laws of history and matter or, if you like, of Marx,
and any place that men can live they'll someday make a home that's
       pretty grand.

[Africa, 1944]

Pedimonte

(unfinished)

Peace once possessed this land outright; the brown Volturno
Is a tenant, and walled. A life only stays by squatter's right;
Miles are no test of measurement but what an ox will pace
And time is what he drags; and curfew comes directly with the night;
And Pedimonte where we are is just another name for peace.

And if you call the mountains stately white-crowned queens,
Then the valley follows flowing as a lovely trailing dress
Embroidered at the foot with bricked and terraced olive-groves;
And round the vineyards and the cottages a restfulness
That only more than many centuries of labour gives.

The lanes are what I love; they seem the only path I'd care
To take to England, – rutted and sunk by wear, the roots
Of trees spill in among the lizards and the violets; deep
And narrow, so that tanks would have to take some other route,
Although there's room enough for several oxen or a jeep.

I'd like to walk along these lanes in the scent of the sun
Beside the pink anemones and lemon trees, and watch
The track get wide and grassy, and the flowers become
Hawthorn and blackthorn and crabapple, until I reach
The welling hills of Wycombe and the lanes of Buckingham.

Peace was blindfolded and shot and left to rot in a lane
Some time back. A life has not sorted out her dead
Yet, and got them from the wreck and plaster. Cassino
Sends down gusty gunfire in each clot of wind. Instead
Of stars we have the ghastly nightlights of Cassino.

Yet there's no contrast; peace and murder are the fruit and flower
Of one tree, and freedom is its name. And Englishmen
Are fighting at Cassino for such lanes as these, although the path
Is not through them; and so when we go up to meet the guns
We'll know that peace is dangerous, but worth the risk of death.

[1944]

This poem was part of a letter to his parents, in which he wrote:

I felt as if I was walking on air the whole time. Climbing up into the mountains under which we lived to where the croci flowered on the edge of the snow; walking up and down to the mess along deep sunken lanes of violets and cyclamen leaves; the lizards in all the hedges, so frequent that wherever you walked there was a continual rustling beside you; the white cottages with lemon trees growing up them, and rich white oxen living in the downstairs rooms; and then the sudden red flaming of the fields when the gladioli flowered. Whenever I breathed there seemed to be a great fragrance in the air; it was such a change from the indifferent sequence of olive-groves, rocks and scrub that made up the countryside in North Africa. I wrote a poem at the time which I never sent you because I was not satisfied with it, and because it had two more verses at the end which were quite remarkably bad and were awaiting revision. Here it is – called 'Pedimonte'. [The] last line wasn't true anyway, as the nights were fine there, – not as bright as the African nights it is true, but delightful in other ways, and for several days we had the magnificent spectacle of Vesuvius in eruption to the south, throwing up fireballs and tearing little fissures of mauve gassy light in the darkness, a long way away. And so on for another verse, even more painful. Still perhaps I shall work on it sometimes, and make something of it, to remember those weeks by.

Song for 1945

Come, make your mind up, friend, make up your mind.
The fiery earth is turning once again
And fires are kindling in the bones of men.
Make up your mind, man, or get left behind.

Get up, man, stand up, stand, you Englishman!
Oh yes, I know once more the juggler sun
Will toss about the star we stand upon;
Earth will behave as it has always done, –

And yet whatever the huge heavens do,
Whether the night runs white or day drains black,
Never an age of turning will bring back
This time which history has brought us to.

So make your mind up, man, go shake your head.
We have less time to spend while you decide
Than the moon spends in gathering the tide.
For men are marching, men are lying dead

About us, brother, lying dead tonight.
And while the rich sit diceing for the poor
A wind from Europe batters at the door.
Get up, man, stand up, rouse yourself to fight,

For if you join us now we'll never stop.
Have done with talking. It is getting late, –
The sun drags time around and will not wait.
Get into step, friend, get yourself in step!

[Written in the New Year and published in *Our Time*, February 1945]

Casola Valensio: The Cat

I'm sure no love of ours had kept her there
After her master left. She hid herself from sight
By day. She seemed to know that men had ceased to care
For company. So she patrolled, like us, at night,
And often in the dark we started up in fright,
Thinking she was the enemy inside our wire.
But still we let her be, until she tripped a flare,
And spent its light, and showed the Germans where we were.

I ordered that the cat be shot. 'There is no time
In war to exhaust one's heart on animals,' I said,
'What is a shell-torn forest to one shattered home?
This wretched cat before a human life?' I said.
'The longer that she lives the sooner we'll be dead.
Besides, she'll serve to give your marksmanship a check.'
So we waited. And the next time that she came
A man fired, wounding the creature in the neck.

She cried and all night wandered crying in the snow.
Her blood thawed crimson patches in the bitter white.
And still we heard her weakening below
Until the soldiers' faces wasted into white
And misting pity misinformed the sentries' sight,
Because of her complaint who wandered to and fro
And was distressed by forces which she could not know
And in her time of dying had no place to go.

War, when a soldier dies, his comrades turn away
Their eyes and shut their hearts. There is no man who'd dare
Consider on the thing and still maintain the day.
It is set by for remembering in a future year.
And so it was this sorrow entered unaware
And vanquished us. And we were half-ashamed to show
Such pity for a creature we set out to slay.
She was the waste of Europe, crying in the snow.

[Grassina, February 1945]

Approach March, Last Offensive

May this offensive mean some end at last!
Time and again the fascists have been beaten back
And our avenging armies, growing in might,
Have battled down converging roads, until it seems
The end has grown remote with our civilian dreams
And we'll be everlastingly condemned to fight.
And yet this evening, watching my division spreading past –
A vast armoured city moving on tracks –

I triumph in our strength. The convoy lights
Outstare the stars, and like a never-ending stream
Of evidence for final victory, the bragging tanks
Make powder of the road. Burnt fumes and dust
Become a fragrance to us, and we give our thanks
For these abundant means since end they must.

[Cesana, April 1945]

Untitled

Mother, why do you wear that disaffected look?
Such grief is quite extremist, when you consider
Your first-born son was always a rank outsider
And hardly worth the expense of the rusty hook

We hung him from. Now consider instead
The terms of my duty, which is hardly pleasant
With prices what they are – one penny a peasant,
Tuppence a worker – and, since the severing of heads

Has been forbidden by the Liberal Minister
In deference to western practice, we must take
Each prisoner alive for questioning. So we can't fake
Some unoffending head and make it sinister

And save our trouble (all heads are much alike,
Lawyer or fisherman or cook, once they are severed,
Black from travel, dust in the eye-sockets, covered
In blood and spittle), sticking like the shrike

Does on his thorns our larder in the villages.
Why be distressed? One brigand, as I said,
Is much like any other. This one, being dead,
Is twice a brigand, since he brutally pillages

Your cracking heart. Order must be preserved.
The rope was twitching only for your good.
And even (lest we should be misunderstood
In certain quarters) all forms have been observed

Perfectly. The process of prosecution
Accorded with that which Western Democracy follows.
A priest with a hymnbook stood beside the gallows.
A British Observer attended the execution.

The Senate authorised a loan for the purchase of rope
And an accredited hangman cut him down.

Now, lest by a miracle your withered womb
Should nourish more extremists, your reviving hope
Of progeny be granted (can we overlook
You were accomplice in the crime?) I'll trouble you
To pack and follow me.

> *Smile, mother, damn you,*
Or I'll gouge out that disaffected look.

[1945]

New Fashions

*'The fashion houses, who have been denied Paris fashions for
four years, are hoping they will reach the freed city in time to
secure the "freedom" and "victory" dress designs which will
sweep the women's world this winter... If we can get back
soon we shall be able to resume where we left off. Fashions
out of Paris this winter should be very striking indeed.'*

PRESS REPORT, 4 SEPTEMBER 1944

Rejoice! For, while designing men
Followed their fashions, fought and found
Them under grass or underground,
Still lived La Mode Parisienne.

And with the flag of freedom furled,
O, still the long-established firms
Designed the panties, zips and perms
To re-invade the women's world.

Modom must suit this style of hair –
'La Libération du Caen';
This hat, à petites gouttes de sang,
The 'Mort à Pucheau' brassière.

Modom would be très chic, très sage
To grace this robe – 'Gloire de Maquis'.
For lipstick – 'Ennemis Vaincus'.
For scent – 'Soupçon de Sabotage'.

Modom should view our line in veils
Inspired in mourning for Laval;
Our corset – 'Candeur de De Gaulle';
Our bath-salts – 'Odours of Marseilles'.

And these creations, tant risquées,
Recall Grenoble and Haute Savoie.
This rouge is named 'Thorez et Toi'.
For nails, the tint 'Carnage au Pays'.

Modom's advised to throw off black
And dance with jackboot modes in shoes
And jitter to the Pétain blues.
The Flanders poppies are come back

So wear a grave-cloth as a cape
And dance with pennies in your eyes.
O, what a wealth a war supplies, –
New tastes in riding-whips and rape,

And Modom must lay bare her charms
Since Freedom is not shy or vague.
The Winged Victory's the vogue, –
Modom *must* chop off her arms!

[1945]

Three Love Poems

I

There are more men among our night,
Admirers, trespassing, who share
Your favours, loosening your dress.
As my astonished fingers press
Your begging breasts or tell your hair
I am outnumbered. The white

    Thronged cemeteries of Europe stare,
    Their thickset eyes on us. So
    Will they lie anonymous while we
    Shape our identity together. So
    They must ever rest. So let them be

Keeping straight discipline until
Time overturns. We have no choice
But to be fortunate tonight.

    And yet they intersperse the moment still,
    Jostling your body, speechless in my voice.
    I am afraid to suffer this delight
    Which once an army waiting first light
    Saw, evanescent in the morning's veil, –
    Freshwater English chalice, chosen grail.

II

Your nakedness, my just reward
For hoarding what my comrades lack,
Blood in my body. Coward
One time perhaps, or merely luck

    Ducking my head. Behind your eyes,
    Its girders jettisoning flame,
    Incendiary London lies.
    Murder, scrawling across my name
    Endorsement, shot with the same gun
    Some German heart in Italy

My heart which should have pitied her.
Nor can I estimate my gain,
Surrender to you totally,
It is sufficient to be here

    Alive, delighting I am animal
    And you are animal, with ale-brown hair,
    Plunder on your white shoulders, prodigal,
    Splendidly loosed, all plenty settled there.
    Learning these spendthrift lessons, claim release
    Long overdue. This school should teach us peace...

III

Or armistice, some time to heal,
Each reaching in our human space
The five dimensions of our love.
We'll counterspin a richer whole
Threading my anger with your grace.
We have no other way to live

> While history treads down the stairs,
> Jutting long shadows on our plain.
> They are insensate as the stars.
> Their dreaming is in what we do.
> Our action is their only gain.
> My love, as I lie down with you
> Wheatlands converse in the Ukraine
> And some Sicilian vineyard stirs

And you, my love, are girlfriend comrade lass
Within an army's arms, obeying this
Intemperate imperative to kiss,
Reaping that plenty in. Though we are thus
Sad harvesters, our harvest's vast. Not less
But fiercer loving must reveal their loss.

[1946]

Chemical Works

I *The Machines*

Ammonia, essence of lavender, chalk.

Talk,
machines, talk, talk,
you are the ones who do the talking.

Bawling at first, metal in mutiny,
wrestling musclemen, seeking punishers,
growling cudgeling struggling marauders
hurting and mauling on opposing causes
murderers
      henchmen
          hooligans
              howling
menacing and pummeling locking interlocking
hubbub of driving belts grouse of gearing
pelting
      cheering
          knocking at nerves
beyond endurance...
              Pauses.
Settles respectably into the subconscious
conditioning the will to the method of warning
dowsing the instincts, hypnotising hearing,
relaxing the animal heart,
             returning
with suave impeccable meticulous precision
civilised adjusted lubricated rhythm
clubmen businessmen men in possession
rocking their jaws with repetitive assurance
in skull-like fixity of conversation
tapping with slack and rattling fingers
nodding to each other, courteously bending
the scooped-out vacancy of automatic heads.

Bowing and condescending,
                    mocking
the awkward colloquialisms of walking boots
the inadequate dialect of human breathing
the slangy toil of unregulated hearts

the inefficient soil on the slats of chalk.

II *The Girls*

O for an end to the monotone of school,
Running round for Mum and the neighbour's condescension.
There's more in life than in a simple equation.
There's Jean in Woolworth's, Sally at the mill,
Trams and cosmetics, the conquest of skill
In setting your hair or minding a machine.
There's lights at night, the electric fear of Hell,
A plastic raincoat and a fifth dimension.
There's money enough to buy whatever the cinemas sell
And the singular convention of being sixteen.

For a tall man at the gates, O, with cream in his hair
And a tight two-seater. For a rich baritone
And 'Pardon me, lady...' or 'Madam, if you please...'
For a voice to whisper 'Honey, now you're here
I'll never let you go. You'll never go back there.'
O for a break of some sort, some sort of release,
And a curse O curse a curse upon the world
That has made a canker of desire of the sun,
That there's so little point in being twenty-one,
That I should be so early aware of growing old.

Forget about the orange-blossom, never mind the priest
But give me a chance. They've done for my skin
But my figure's still OK. O give me at least
An ordinary fellow with average pay,
A chance of having children before it gets too late,
A basement room and a washing-day.
There's not much left to lose at twenty-eight.
O change me for a moment! Let me in
Past the commissionaire by the Golden Gate
At least to the giddy vaults of technicolour sin.

O for a minor accident and a broad-shouldered pension!
But the company would win. I'm thirty-seven.
There isn't a schedule to assess my compensation.
Twelve years at piecework tore my youth to tatters.
My womanhood has leaked away in titters.
But what's the point in adding up these sums?

O grant me only this, O grant me, heaven,
Not any unpossible love, no, no unlikely bliss
But something somehow to get me out of this
Before the final suitor with his dark proposal comes.

III *Formula and Product*

Time's early mixing room
where world and girl begun:
her flesh potential in the sulphurous fire
and spirit was implicit in the loam.
Abrasion (was it?), brawn of sun
rubbed on the lukewarm mud, inflamed the dark
into a pinhead spark –
matter in conflagration, appetite, desire,

impetus and skill,
technique and mastery,
burning the icy continents inside
the chalky tumult of the carried skull.
O issue of all history
out of that arbitrary act of sun!
What have we done
to give this unspent match, this brushwood for a bride,

firm-footed seventeen,
all matter most aware,
into these forks and parallels of steel?
Caging her sweet age here with a machine,
her proud tread, head-of-tinder hair:
coating the hunger of her open lung:
letting go youth among
eight-hour attrition of re-iterating wheels.

And what is physical
ammonia does burn out:
chalk slows her veins and sulphur pits her skin.
What happens only once (and after all
earth, air, has rocked to bring about)
O flesh of maid and sensuous consciousness
each day made less,
ashes for profit, agony in tins.

[1947]

Yugoslav Partisan: To the Western World

             – How many times we stood
Against the clammy wall of dawn/claimed
Death among knocking bullets death
And freedom
             curse on curse
In the last cough of our hearts, clutching
Hate like a thumb in our hands. Philosophers
Of action/dung
On our clothes/changing ourselves
With guns. And hunger-struck
We stuck our clenched fists in our stomachs
Sucked our will/went on till death
(Comic as meat on a hook or black
Festering/broken-backed /swollen in mud)
Confirmed the dialectics of our dignity.
Seeing the white sanity of our own snows
So puddled and writ/crimson with anti-fascist blood
Society could no more be illiterate.
We learned to read and act.

             – Go and call conferences
Thump the ballot-box /write books
Draw inferences from your own diseases.
Rummage in libraries for freedom's definition.
Ask astrologers.
Wet your own nest and croak and flap
Your spattered plumage like an army.
Write notes of protest. Test
Your atom-bombs on coral atolls.
Do what relieves you best.

Crawled over by lice /peopling every seam of us
Almost ashamed to look /we
Fashioned a new concept of man
Fleshed by our frost-bite/born
In the confinement of our comradeship.

We have become involved
In history, whose granite skull
No rock can crush, whose eyes
Fire can't put out /nor can the torturer
With all his clinical skill
            skinning its fingernails
Make it retract one fact about us.

            Once again
Death to the fascists, freedom to the people!
We have accomplished all we willed.
We've come of age in consciousness/won
Mastery of ourselves/proved stronger than
Flint fire shot frost hemp hail steel
                        and
Today we build
            a man stronger than man.

[1948, punctuation as in the manuscript. A version
of this poem, abbreviated by the editor, appeared
in *The Voice of Scotland,* June 1948.]

The Place Called Choice

I

Crime and compassion, then, statistics, ecstasy,
Struck like a match from chaos. It's all an accident:
This town beneath me meaning no more than stonecrop,
Lichen of banks and offices: fungus on a stone wall,
Spawning into the night a pretty stitchwork of lights
Like swarming midget spiders, bringing someone money.
Widows and acrobats, clowns, suicides:
It's all in the luck of the draw. Man makes what he can get.
The kids play at bandits. Blood issues on the speedway.
The gunmen point from the hoardings, indicating manhood:
Virility slouching in a soft hat and an oil-stained raincoat,
Getting girls at a bargain, going loaded to the cash-tills,
Educating the young in the ethics of business.
The weak get cracked like grapeseed, chewed into digits.
On the corner by the Palace
Without malice or logic
Death waits in a slumped indifferent posture,
Sticking his knuckles in the eyes of all comers.

The applewood is black, bearing fruit at the back of mills.
At Manchester you can find a forgotten half-acre of gravestones,
The grey light blocked by the utilitarian chapel,
The Mechanics Institute, the condemned back-to-back terraces.
Soot settles on the cemetery, assuaging its chemical hunger,
Adjusting the stone accounts, writing off our grandparents' losses.
A good plot lost to the dairyman, the jerry-builder, now to all memory
Except of the local antiquaries, muffled in Sunday's habit,
Pacing between tilted crosses, tracing some local worthy:

Or once in a leap-year some American returning
To hunt up his ancestors, hoots into the dark passage-way,
Enters the wrought-iron creaking gates. Rain on the headstones
Where Jones the Chartist is buried.

     Wind crosses the marshes,
Fowey, the Cinque Ports, a sand-bar across an estuary:
Silt, mudflats, wormcasts, black posts, rushes, saltings,

Nets rotting in a brackish inlet, a Viking war-way:
The neglected sea-groyne, cork-floats, tar, corrupting bladder wrack.
The scavenging gull and the shag lime the clipper's keel
Where picnic-makers throw refuse, sucked half under in sand.

Or buried in a bookshop in an unfrequented quarter –
Bristol, perhaps, or Nottingham – the stack marked down to sixpence,
The dust rarely disturbed: Cobbett's paper, yellow at the edges;
The *New Moral World*; the *Black Dwarf*; Cooper; Bradlaugh.
A find for some collector, more stuffing for a thesis.
Or in the reference library, entombed in the white card-index,
Paine's *Rights of Man* which once in some high Pennine valley
The weaver at his handloom, straining by rushlight, read.

Wind crosses the moors. The valley of the last wolf.
Old iron workings. Micre. Quartz. The monotonous peatbog –
Black roots, ling, harebell, the wet relics of a forest.
The gutted stannary. Scrub oak on the old encampment,
Brambles and st-john's-wort. Among the chalk-bits and pellets,
The droppings of rabbits, a shred of pottery, a flint, a coin.

Or with more grace at Burford, integral with Cotswold stone,
Entering the ceremony of cottages, sweet williams and crown imperial,
Buried among neighbours and labourers, the Leveller corporals.
Riding by night the Roundheads forded the river –
Fifty miles since dawn, Fairfax and Cromwell –
Rested in water-meadows among frog-cup and loddon lily:
Found them and rode them down, their doublets still unbelted,
Drowsy at midnight, damp cramping their hips, fatigue
Of freedom's parturition, of a hidden understanding
Nudging their dreams. Damage of horses
Sundering the darkness – sudden clamour of orders –
Tinder-boxes – odour of burned powder, garlic.
Then on the leads time enough for meditation.
Later, in the churchyard –
The round-dance come to an end, the children hailed indoors –
Hard determination was needed for that death in full daylight,
Looking at the muskets marking their target,
The soldiers torn in their duty…

Wind crosses the cities,
Driving the rain under doors, sweeping the housing estates,
Kicking with ten-league boots at the evening racing special,
The pools slip, the Woodbine carton, the plain cover for contraceptives,
Clapping the corrugated sheets on the roof of the garage,
Sluicing the wrecker's yard, the back-axles, the sodden cardboard:
Rusted nails, brake-linings, tyres, half-bricks, oddments.

– And now squats in the knotted core of this town
Among the keening smokestacks, the megalithic condensers,
The engines shunting in the yards, the dark bulk
And lighted swarm of the mills. And the wide-eyed child
Listens to the wail in the guttering, watches the street-lamp
Spill and people the walls with shadows, guardsmen, bandits:
The cocked stance of the gunman, the slouched shape on the corner –
Sensing enemies as human – the spy and the hunched-backed miser –
Never thinking for a moment of the wind at the door, the wolf…

Wind that is geological time, eraser of familiar landmarks,
Opposing the gait and strike of strata, scouring the faults:
Incessant commentator, stalking the peaks and hursts,
Scanning the smoke of valleys and the straddled cities…
                    Across the alluvial gravel,
Over the Swanscombe skull, crunched among ammonites and shells:
Over the tiny crustacea, the bric-a-brac of chalk –
First cousins to our father
Who lies crouched in the abandoned road of memory
Clutching in his stone fist a charm against the centuries:
Trawling the turfs of Fosberry with a net of shadows,
Vaulting the Countless Stones, the barrows, the temple to Mithras,
Bursting the hinges of Stonehenge and entering on Halifax,
Howling in the eyeteeth of a boar, through the saurian's crutch:
Harrowing our bones now and whatever bones went before us:
Wind, crossing peaty headlands,
Crying in pylons,
Questioning the conscience of this island,
Stuck like a white fishbone in the chops of the Atlantic –

If you had suffered
In your own person the pain of the spine's erection:
The brain stretching within the skull, ache of the widening eyes:
Pressed south by that tonnage of ice, had your white hide
Sliced into blood by the sabre of the biting tiger,
And now, stooping to put out the bottles on your doorstep,
Or dropping the sports page for a moment to stir the fire,
Suddenly heard that question in the wheel of your ear –
The wash of the sea in the shell, the wet acres, the wind ...

Would you recall for a moment your figure on the earthwork,
Sweating in brown firelight, hacking with shaped antlers,
Throwing up a wall against tall oncoming strangers:
And the late watch on the dyke while the infernal nightjar
Kept scarring the silence and startling the sentries:
That night on the Sangro
Waiting with corked face and vine-leaves in your helmet
For the canvas boat to be launched among hanging flares?

Would you pause and consider
Whether anything was lacking, whether all was in order,
Or some important engagement might have slipped your memory –
Some dues outstanding to a half-remembered union?
Sensing within that interthreading of workshops;
In the intricate by-ways and slips between the Palace,
The speedway, the Lyric, and the accountant's offices
Some human bond more strict than the bonds of money,
Warmer, it may be supposed, but more exacting?

England in the grip of suave, competent killers;
Her will weakened by an ethic of money-spiders
And all the cant and claptrap of a vicious individualism,
Masking the lurking coshboys, the slouching gunmen,
Letting in the agents of the ancient antagonist.
Sand silts the narrow roads,
Making obsolete the heroic charts, the old markers of feeling.
The couch-grass and the plantain obscure the white landmarks
Of a culture down on its luck, of a nation of hawkers.
The wind knocks for an entry, the waste encroaches,
And on the Pennine uplands
The Chartists march no more with their pikes and torches.

England, buried somewhere under bricks, oddments, worn tyres:
Under the shady transactions clinched in the flashy roadhouse:
Buried with Arnald and Lockyer: with Holberry: with Linell:
With the charred bodies of the pieceners scorched in the weaving-shed:
With the victims of anthrax: in the back courtyards of Bradford
Where the applewood is black, bearing fruit by the oldest mills:
Stupefied in the smoke of Sheffield, sullen in Derbyshire,
Raking up old grievances and grousing in East London –
Recall the old challenge
Which each generation has no choice but to master:
Flint, bronze, and iron, and the human union –

Or you, on your doorstep,
Turning back to mumble your private solutions,
You will not avoid the slumped figure on the corner:
On the moors of space from the tree of your skeleton
Noosed in your timid and unrealised existence
You will swing in the winds of your death for ever.

II

The night was full of heaving, matter in labour,
Sucking the vacuum in, expelling at last
With anxious love the tiny identical spawn:
Then vegetables with feelers, climbing toadstools,
Long-haired arachnids, egg-laying creatures
The size of a bank. Beneath the accountant's office
We found the tusks and gills, the horny clashing scales,
And reconstructed the slope and swarm of its carriage –
The brain in the base of the tail and the skull like a teacup.
This was next morning. But that night
At every window was the breath of clawed beasts.

At dawn the noise diminished. Give thanks for that.
We did give thanks, with thirty children's blood,
And their bright heads when dried might keep the demons out,
Two men must carry the carved bug of emerald
Which brought our crops fruition, with due sacrifice.
The first light shamed the creatures to the woods,
But still we could see little through the mist
Except for those stone images with beaks
And the terrible ten-armed and helmeted gods.

At nine the Greeks went out, helmeted and cruel.
They came back cruel and helmeted, but radiant.
The place (they said) was good. More sacrifice.
And so, shortly before ten, the men of business
Issued out from the house to set the place in order.

A lot needed attention. Those heathen idols
Were quite unsuited to a man with his professions.
The carved bug went, the cannon did much more.
He created from his rib a well-organised god
With regular office-hours and remarkable files.
It was quite safe to go out now. At half-past ten
The maid banged the gong and we gathered in the drawing-room.
We held a brief service of prayer and thanksgiving.

We had all got around the table for elevenses
When – quite suddenly – matter opened its jaws and retched,
Fetching up a great belch in the shape of a mushroom
With curly rootstrings of fire eye-sockets pus
Ricestraw red with abortions cots full of scabs.

Nothing quite so big as this had happened before.
The doorstep was crowded. The distress was painful.
The headline blew its nose and shuffled uneasily.
The concepts of dignity coughed in their hands discreetly.
The treatise on ethics cried 'ah love oh pity'
And went up to bed. The well-adjusted god
Came down in person, flatulent with forgiveness.
For minutes afterwards the sermons were in mourning.

But no one had done it. The alibis were perfect.
All were indoors – no one had left the house.
Some suspicion, it is true, fell upon the scientist
Who was rumoured to keep something secret in his lab,
But those who had seen it said the story was nonsense:
He kept it as a pet. The bug was innocent.

The matter stood there. The issue was undecided.
It was not my line of business. I went back to my room.
But I felt, somehow, uneasy. I kept looking at the clock...
At five to twelve there broke in at my door
That sandalled runner wet from Marathon,
Leaping the alluvial gravel, skirting the chalk-pit,
Fording the centuries, fresh-scarred from Stalingrad,
Shaking me by the pulse, crying to wake the house:
'Stand to your life! About you, brother, look!'

I looked and the ethics crawled beneath the skirting:
The concepts fell apart and swarmed with gaols:
The emerald headlines bulged with sacrificial blood,
The statesmen wore bright heads to keep the fiend at bay.
Not once or twice only, but everywhere I looked
The putrescence of ideology suppurating its pious pus.

Defilement of life! From each denial,
From the timid evasions and privacies of the good,
From the saurian's crutch, the successful man of business,
The pointed tool of the gunman,
From the lusting speedway, from each sale to the bank
Of the bonds of human choice, there issues this spawn,
Swarming the yard of the world like midget spiders,
Spawn of that fungus settling on every city,
On the walls, the cathedrals, climbing the keening smokestacks,
Drifting on every sill, waiting there to germinate:
To fetch our house up in one belch.

Already the windows are shut, the children hailed indoors.
We wait together in the unnatural darkness
While that god forms outside in the shape of a mushroom
With vast blood-wrinkled spoor on the windswept snow.

And now it leans over us, misting the panes with its breath,
Sucking our house back into vacuous matter,
Helmeted and beaked, clashing its great scales,
Claws scratching on the slates, looking in with bleak stone eyes.

III

What should a poet say?
Poet, a pretty thing.
Philatelist of words,
Playing with sets of rhyme,
Sticking in kings and birds,

Sensing behind the wall
And the technicolour murals
The silverfishes crawl
Nests of digits mate,
Throughout the state
A stench of blocked morals
And at the top of all
The wittol and the stall?

Say first we stand upon
A tributary star,
Issue of chaos, one
In a swarming universe.
Say next that life began
As accidental spawn
Of some atomic war
Within the changing sun.
And last declare that man
(All changing matter alone)
Grew taller than his nurse –
Air, water, stone –
Arose and challenged change,
Chaining the atoms down

But found within his soul
A civil war begun
And felt within his heart
The seeds of fission spawn
Till matter broke apart
Flaming from pole to pole
The star fell in the sun

And while the poet sat
Turning the album of time
Sticking in this and that
To make a set of rhyme
Swarming chaos took
The poet and his book.

*

We are each way defined –
We stand on the crust of a star
Turning about a coal,
Eternity's wind behind
Infinity's moors before.
Man is what he has made,
Carving himself a soul
With bone and cutting blade.
The flint and teaching spade
Revealing what we are.
From each encounter with matter
Man and his needs have grown:
Air, stone, and water
Thought to limit his needs,
But out of the water came wisdom
And song came out of the stone.
First of all I declare
That man is changed by his deeds,
And all within his kingdom
Is stone, water, air

Transformed into a fire
Lighting the moors and blown
By every tempest higher
Until air, water, and stone
In the furnace of the mind
Are changed into desire
And all things are defined.

*

I stand upon this hurst
Above the straddled town,
Considering water and air
And fire at the core of stone,
Calling to mind the first
Flint arrowhead, shaped antler –
Clumsily fashioned stuff
To master wolf or bear,
And yet it was matter enough
To make man come aware
Of desire and knowledge, vast
As the megalithic altar
Cast from the stuff of his thought:
I stand amazed at the past –
All flint, bone, have taught:
Considering how the steel,
Oil and teaching steam
Reveal unknown desires,
New ways to act and feel –
The fractured atoms seem
In their creating fires
Already to meet and plan
A megalithic man.

It's time to speak one's mind.
I'm sick of an 'anxious age'.
I am fed to the teeth with the cant
Of 'guilt' and original sin.
From all the fires that raged
In England's youth I find
A grocer's timid candle
Is all that is left behind:
And life being unassuaged
By the fuel of cant and cash
Consumes us in the flames
Of unfulfilled desire
Down to sarcastic ash
And threatens to disown
Fire with terrible fire,
Air, water, and stone
Resume what was their own.

Whatever evil there is
I declare was first let in
By timid men with candles
And abstract talk of sin.
Man is what he has made,
Chipping bone with bone,
Shaping the teaching spade:
Urged by his human needs
Changes the world, and then
Transfigured by his deeds,
Changes necessity,
Becoming whole and free.

I stand upon the earth
And watch the hursts of space,
And at last I raise my voice
In the teeth of the swarming wind:
I declare that man has choice
Discovered in that place
Of human action where
Necessity meets desire,
And moors and questioning wind,
Water, stone, and air,
Transfigured in the soul,
Can be changed to human fire
Which man, becoming whole,
Will order and control.

IV

Crime and compassion, then, statistics, ecstasy,
But mostly crime. At first the fat Cistercians
Engrossing the farms with love. Rascals like Hawkins,
Their sloops steaming with slaves, trading in bibles –
But valiant men in their way, men to encounter the wind.
Then Cromwell with his chaplain, slaying at Burford
Buff-coated passion, was still a fit antagonist,
Swearing by Property and Christ, an honest hypocrite.

Next came the jolly vicar with his sensitive daughters.
The weavers starved in their looms. Silicosis, anthrax:
The hunch-backed children, the pieceners charred in the mills:
Black mud and standing water, the craters of Passchendaele,
Men making good with guns. And all those accidents
Fetched up by benevolent progress. Last, that race
Of well-adjusted masters, victims of every wind,
The bloody spoor in the snow, the monster of stone.

Standing above the lamplit town I watch this crime,
Cruel and beaked, crushing all comprehension,
Killing whole streets of men, sticking his horny knuckles
In the eyes of whoever comes. Man, who is changed by his hands,
Evolved the man of business, within whose mind
The clawed beast of possession gnawed all bonds until
Man fell apart, and split from self to self,
The acquisitive brain cutting off the creative hands.

Now crime, compassion, have reached the place called choice.
I hear at last the voice of resolution, loud
From the flagstones and setts, the commons engrossed for sheep,
From the mullioned windows, the lighted bulk of the mills,
And the living killed in their streets. In the frost-blue flames
Of the handloom weaver's rushlight the heroic shadows leap:
Mellor at Cartwright's mill: Jones on the hustings: names
That merge with anonymous shadows, shaping that man who crowds

Every room of the human house, opens the windows, stands
Warming the winds of space at his compassionate hands.

[Halifax, October–December 1950]

SHORT POEMS

(1952-1973)

Declarations of Love

(for Dorothy)

I

I saw her bend over my son in the garden,
And the child turned suddenly and shouted at the snow.
That was enough to set these sensual rhythms swaying
Till all the rooms of reason rang: and I, above,
Saw words, like dancers, in their hundred motions go
Among the patterns which the fiddlers were playing,
And one recurring word came past, which I called 'Love'.

But the word caught cold and died, becoming coin,
Clacking the disks of the clockwork-box called 'Sex'.
I could not see her for close-ups and patent lipsticks,
And the air crooned with a male choir of echoes,
Bumming their public list all over the acoustics.

Next, and at night, I took on like a glove
Her white and mortal beauty, till the gestures of her kind –
Ness grew so great, they could no longer be contained
Within the latched concerns of my delighting mind.
And all these years of silence stirred within my lung,
And, kicking on my tongue, cried 'Love'.

But the bright boys took away the word and cut it open.
They couldn't find its name in the index of perversions,
So they put it in a tin with some rosaries and verses
And sent it to a brothel to comfort sinning persons.
There was bickering about it when they came to look,
But all of them agreed it were better born unspoken.

O, we broke out from these dusty places, to the world
Of human action where all notable things are done.
The sun was driven by our shadows all day long.
Because we willed it so, our hands were full of doves.
Trees grew, because we planted them. Children and songs
Climbed in the olive-trees of hope, until, in unison,
We lost all shame, and in the public fields we shouted 'Love'.

71

But the sun dropped off its stalk into black miles of water.
The birds mobbed us like owls. The trees and children fled,
Screaming, to the dead heathlands and the howling moors.

And the word, like a foul sorcerer, was groping on our bed,
Intoning false and pious spells, which, starting into wars,
Threw down its glacial shadow on us, prophesying parting.

II

My love, the earliest poets knew
That man was other than animal,
And woman was half man, half fire:
And, in the union of the two,
The double bridge of sex and sense
Spanning the gulf of identity
Brought the opposing capitals
Into a crowning unity.
Straddling the chasm of personal death,
The social buildings, dome and spire,
Composed a city common to each,
Reaching the heights where both aspire.
O, is it my own incompetence,
That you, who quicken my desire
With each inflexion of your breath,
Confirming all I read or heard –
Find me incapable of speech,
And picking quarrels with a word?

Or has the word, through too much use
In stuffing every trivial hole
Of intellectual fear and hate –
Daubing the poster's self-abuse,
Employed among the means of state
By every butcher in a stole, –
Dissolved into its component dust,
The calculating rational soul,
The functional urges of animal lust?

And when this special kindness still
Brushes the entrance to our hearts,
Suggesting we are human yet,
We squash the word upon the sill,
Dead as a wasp: or else must set
Ourselves to talk by different arts,
And fashion a silent alphabet?

III

Love, they said, and ordered in the armour of possession.
Love, they said, annexing their children as dependencies.
Love, they said, scuffling among the Korean crossbones.
Love, they said, love, as they cuddled in their jealous trenches.
Making incense on their souls under the dynasty of cordite.

Forgive me. I had almost said, this word is carrion.
Sold up our lyrical inheritance, gone croaking like a crow,
Clapping with verminous wings and cawing at their crookedness,
And (if they hadn't found me meat) I would no more have spoken.

That was my road. But as I moved to go
I saw you in the garden, in the summer of your senses,
And our son flushed with shouting, who, two years ago
Crawled in the grass, kicked on his back
The year before, before that was no son at all.
And then you laughed at me, and said, Come out into the snow.

Conversions fall like this, I think. Such facts as these
Grow into revolutions, so that, in crying out your name
I must cry out defiance on all treacheries,
Throw down their alphabets and purge their subtle schools of shame.

O, in the killing air, since I first learned to speak,
They've had their soldiers out. And, listening in the dark,
I've heard their horsemen riding down the weak.
I think I never knew the child that did not bear some mark.

73

And now at last I find my voice, my singing voice of rage.
O let the old vocabularies join the bitter dance!
I am moved to declare against this unjust butchering age.
Against Wellington, Meinau, Rhodes, MacArthur – all
The licensed, decorated killers, who, like cocks
Roost with their bloody spurs within the orthodox,
And (with each dawn) fly out and crow from every fence
And cry down any air of innocence.

And I affirm that word, which, should we let it fall,
Faith or ingratitude, no other word can live
Which stakes our social world, holds back the lurching animal,
I take our son in my arms. I kiss you and plead my love.

[1952]

In Praise of Hangmen

How can we other than
Honour that man
Who undertakes this social trust
Since someone must?

How much more honour then
To all those dedicated men
Who saved society
By rope and calumny.

So giving honour we
Who moralise necessity
With slate of sophistry erect
A gibbet of the intellect

And from its foul and abstract rope
Suspend all social hope
Until with swollen tongue
Morality herself is hung.

In whose distended dedicated eyes
All honour dies.

[1956]

Valentine

Ten years your separate face
Has made its casual dent
Beside my own. And still I watch
In ten-year-old astonishment.

Surely I should select
Pity out of the eyes:
The mouth's wide generosity:
Scorn of intellect?

Out of the expedient sky
The neutral sandy air
Blows on our lungs. But still in you
Pity must breathe and cry.

The North drives out the South
And caution's cold sets in:
But neither frost nor compromise
Have cooled your generous mouth.

From sand and ice were born
Lies, inhumanities:
But all are powerless against
Your intellectual scorn.

So I must love the face
Where pity can unite
With generosity and scorn
Into a single grace –

But with a love that yet
Does not undo identity:
May you remain still strange to me,
Still free, still separate.

[1957]

Homage to Tibor Dery

In that unanimous agenda of the good
If he should cough the chair would scowl
If he should smile a point-of-order would
Beat out his poems against the wall.
The seven unctuous sins had each confessed
To sinning in the interest of all.
He was too old to be self-critical.
He took his platform down and left the hall.

He could no more abide the orthodox.
The lifelike leaders melted in their wax:
Grief fringed the servile squares like grass:
The statues stood on water. Public clocks
Forged in the small hours twelve important chimes.
He beat upon his art twelve answering times
And held a mirror up, of splintered glass:
He bent his pulse to pick their textual locks,

Easing the tumblers of the people's blood
Till something clicked, the formulations swung
Slowly apart, and a colloquial flood
Of common, fallible words got out.
The sweaty facts fell out of the statistics,
The active verbs ran to the brutal young:
Shame, pity, indignation, doubt
Broke protocol and stormed the city's tongue.

The turret summed up sternly for the good
In syllables so big they shut the old man up.
Confessions, concrete, quotas, stronger locks –
He knows what they can do. But can
They formulate correctly that lewd flood
And stuff the verbs back in the lexicon,
Replace the chimes within the fractured clocks
Or stand those statues on a plinth of blood?

[1959. *Tibor Dery*, the Hungarian novelist and short story writer, was a
powerful voice of socialist humanism in 1956. After the repression of the
Hungarian insurrection he was silenced and then – in 1959 – imprisoned.]

Homage to Salvador Allende

Well, comrade president, what is there left to say?
Predicted all the way: and buried in the end
Without the benefit of media, before the mass
Could say its newses over you, the cameras
Squat in your wounds and blow them up.

Failure makes you like us, our kind of man,
Killed by our kind: petrol pump patriots;
Loyal executives; most loyal constitutional ladies,
Wed to destroyers, setters-on of jets;
Our kindly patient partner, General Fabius,
Who when he strikes strikes hard, getting us in the guts.
Your face was too much common. Money fled uphill
And cost them in their lives who cost your death.

Your art was always an impossible.
Couldn't you learn, with less than half the votes,
The prose of power, the public man's inflation?
You should have been our age, trading their terms
For something less than half a treachery...

Defective realist, poor loyal sod,
Old silly doctor in a palace on your own,
Knowing the odds were up –
                              Why do you hurt our hearts?

Poetic, Latin man! You do not fall within
Our frames of reference. Transfixed by promises
Pledged to the poor in the high Andean pastures;
The crowd in Santiago; the clasped hand of the metal-worker;
The earnest village schoolmistress, searching your face:
These brought their treaties. You signed them with your life

Which you trade now into myth's ageless reference:
Bolivar, Guevara, Allende. Generous continent!
Accusing hemisphere! But not our kind of men,
As we, back in our prosing beds, stir in our myths,
Recalling such men once... and at Philippi one
Who, having fought and failed, took on a Roman end.

[September 1973]

My Study

King of my freedom here, with every prop
A poet needs – the small hours of the night,
A harvest moon above an English copse...

Backward unrationalised trade, its furthest yet
Technology this typewriter which goes
With flailing arms through the ripe alphabet.

Not even bread the pen is mightier than.
Each in its statutory place the giants yawn:
I blow my mind against their sails and fan

The mills that grind my own necessity.
Oh, royal me! Unpoliced imperial man
And monarch of my incapacity

To aid my helpless comrades as they fall –
Lumumba, Nagy, Allende: alphabet
Apt to our age! In answer to your call

I rush out in this rattling harvester
And thrash you into type. But what I write
Brings down no armoured bans, no Ministers

Of the Interior interrogate.
No one bothers to break in and seize
My verses for subversion of the state:

Even the little dogmas do not bark.
I leave my desk and peer into the world.
Outside the owls are hunting. Dark

Has harvested the moon. Imperial eyes
Quarter the ground for fellow creaturehood:
Small as the hour some hunted terror cries.

I go back to my desk. If it could fight
Or dream or mate, what other creature would
Sit making marks on paper through the night?

[September 1973]

INFANT AND EMPEROR

POEMS FOR CHRISTMAS 1983

(for Dorothy)

Annunciation

Nothing will alter because a child is born.
That was a fable. Any pregnant woman would
Savour the oatmeal of her ordinary loss
With some such fabulous story as her time drew on.
Why not throw in some angels with the salt?
It was the other part that the poor understood –
Herod, the Roman magistrates, the cross.

And what if all of it came from a fib?
Warm nights when Mary slipped her quiet bed,
Trespassed across a courtyard, thought up a fine tale
To father that strange love-child in the crib?
The prophets needed miracles. All followed on –
Out of her faithlessness a world of faith ws bred:
The Holy Roman Church, cross-natured Christendom.

But would a thing as ordinary as
A sly adultery have driven Herod wild?
Her love had salt in it – savour of innocence
No Emperor could bear, an aromatic peace
Incensing the whole State, which in its own defence
Drilled fabulous holy armies to deter a child
From being born and kill it when it was.

Nativity

After two thousand years
The star burned out
The kings froze in history
The angels froze in the bible
The mysteries in tinsel
When the shepherds heard voices
They knew it was only the wind.

Out of that arctic legend
Only one escaped
On the high horse of power:
Riding the centuries down
His drumming hooves have harried
All others off the roads.
Now he assumes his hour –

And everything that is
Must crawl beneath
The Herod-coloured sky.
He is the lord of all.

His guards lean on the gates
The road is barred
The bullrushes cut down:
Around the derelict fable
His soldiers tighten their net
And now they beat
Hard on the stable door
Where through the only gate
No magistrate may guard
His enemy leaps in.
He lies in a hollow of straw
Deserted by kings and gods
With only the cows and the sheep
Too silly to get out.

In despite of Herod's curfew
Light stirs in the city.
Because it is pitiful
Pity runs to the child;
Help breaks down the door
Because it has cried for help:
The poor press back the guards

Bringing whatever is needed
Because it is in need
Because the seed must grow
And the child is the seed.

The Inn and the Byre

The well-adjusted shiver by the fire.
The inn is shut. Outside the snowstorm rages
Like realism in the grown-up dark.
Snow drifts about the chiliastic byre
With its familiar gold-leafed images
Warming gilt knuckles at a baby's breath –

Shepherds and anxious messianic kings,
The dear old codgers bringing silly gifts,
The mild-eyed mother, Mary in her blue,
The infant's radiant utopian face –
We have grown neighbourly across the ages
Though we matured in a more serious place

Than Bethlehem. What could a baby do,
Born in this world from that romantic stock?
We know the nature of Leviathan
And have got used to humouring the Beast
And all that rant of power which has put on
God's image in the swill of Holy Loch.

And yet we put this pagan symbol up.
What other emblem is there that might keep
The great disintegrator from the feast?
There's some taboo to it, something It fears
About a new-born infant in its sleep;
Something that draws forgotten visitors –

Frost-bitten mercy, hope pulling off her gloves
Crusted with ice, benighted company
Numb from the cold. And even at the inn
They stir the failing fire, long for release –
Will no one bring the kindling of love,
A sprig of innocence, a twig of peace?

Visitors at the Inn

On the feast of the banknote
Six beggars looked in at the window

Don't turn round said the dancers
Don't look said the ghosts
Draw the blinds said the darkness
One more for the road said the clock

On the feast of the banknote
Six beggars knocked at the window

Dance said the drum
Burn said the lights
Ghosts said the ghosts. Said the clock
I know when to stop

Send for the law said the banknote
Six of the unofficial meek
Are trying to break and enter the earth
Which belongs to my dancers and my drum

Oh blessed the law, holy the ghosts!
When the clock blacks out on the burning road
They shall inherit kingdom come.

The Infant

The ancient gods and goddesses came down
In thunder or in radiance
Impelled by mischief or pursuing lust,
To sit in judgement or to clown
A moment in the mortal dust –
Dancing as dolphins, fucking as a bull,
Assuming for an hour the transience
Of sensual existence, to relieve
The Eternals' tedium of being spiritual.

Great God, what hassle is this in the skies?
How did He fall into this trap?
Some seraph goofed, some cherub must have lost
The true co-ordinates, perhaps
Celestial terminals got crossed
And teleported Him onto a lap
Where now He lies, unable to compose
His googly out-of-focus eyes,
Fist stuck in His mouth, wetting His swaddling clothes.

Poor puny prince of peace, poor helpless sod,
Incarnate deity in agony
With trying to get up his wind –
Humiliating botch-up for a god
Conceived as saviour of mankind
Who cannot even save himself from death!
In pity for his accidental form
God's mother tiptoes to his breath
And pulls the cover up to keep god warm.

Lullaby

Hard was your knocking
    Many months before
Impetuously
    You broke in at my door.

Contracted in my body
    Conceived in the skies
Now at my mercy
    Omnipotence lies:

Strange invader
    From inner space
With hungry mouth
    And wrinkled face!

Childbirth is a pain
    Motherhood a loss –
I shall show the godhead
    Who is the boss:

Talcum his bottom
    And forgive him his sin,
And fasten up god's nappy
    With a safety-pin.

Hush, Master Egotrip!
    Hush, Mister Big!
I will roll you over
    And dance you a jig.
Dance for your mummy
    Dance for her because
God only knows
    Who your daddy was.

Prince of pandemonium,
    Saviour of all,
    Windy boring preacher
    Wrapped in a shawl –

Stop bawling your commandments,
    Shut up and rest,
And sleep full of the sermon
    Of your saviour's breast.

Mother and Child

She looks down, scarcely smiling, as she has always done.
In the road outside horses and men troop past.
A flight of birds disturbs the Emperor's rest –
In order to impound those birds, the generals set
Some murderous pomp and circumstance afoot:
The eagle-headed standards eye her home.
She is beyond the reach of imperial Rome:
If she looked up the child might fret.

It is her calm that drives the Emperor mad.
Why is she looking down? Look to the all-in-one,
High up aloft ineffable, the abstract drum!
She smiles, holding within the circle of her arm
Omens of innocence, a flight of birds,
Insurgent provinces, revolt within the State.
Over the bowels of a bull the priests deliberate ...
She has held the child too long to take alarm.

She warms a growing world, dependent on her milk.
Why should she vex the infant's sleep or stir herself?
She knows the Emperor was suckled by a wolf.
Were she to turn her head and look into the street
Her child might scatter in a flight of birds:
The door would be thrown down, the cradle would be full –
Horsemen and eagles, Emperor, wolf and bull –
And at her breast an empty drum would beat.

The Massacre of the Innocents
(General Herod takes command)

At 02.00 hours the incarnate concept
Of dignity etc. put on its sun-goggles and
Gave the order to advance, since any Friday
Or Monday the millennium might be at hand.

Butter would not melt in that black mouth
I think. These persons were so good
Their halos rolled like hoops among the rubble
And the warm red humbug and the litter of smashed wood.

Mercy was not of this column, being on leave
Whiting some sepulchre, performing those ablutions
Behind the media's lines. But there! She will be back
In time at least to postpone the last executions.

Like the dear hygienic nurse she is, with hands
Smelling of soap, red nails, sweet sister to poor Pity,
Who got stuck in the suburbs under a ram.
At 14.00 hours, anyway, they entered the city.

And Order sent its orderlies about
Lest any disaffected innocents might still be hid –
Not the Old Testament said so much grace
Before and after meat as those guns did.

So many souls were liberated on that day
Out of their cage of skin and freed into the airs
It is curious that a buzzard ate the speeches
And odd that flies should have blown on the prayers.
It was remarked upon. But the turnout was splendid.
'Quite like old times,' the vizor and goggles said.
Now, children, hallowèd be this memorable service,
Which you may meditate upon until you are dead,

When Morality, that immaculate lady, came in season,
And Nobadaddy mounted her in rut,
And she was conceived by him of a white millennium
When all are cleansed of sin, their throats being cut.

An earlier version of this poem was published in the periodical Arena *as 'On the Liberation of Seoul', which took place on 25 September 1950. Edward Thompson prefaced that version with these two epigraphs:*

'American bulldozers had smashed through debris littering the streets, and MacArthur and President Rhee drove to the Capitol. Gen. MacArthur asked all present to join him in the Lord's Prayer. He said that 53 nations had risen up in 'spiritual revulsion against the march of imperialistic Communism', and added: 'By the grace of a merciful Providence our forces, fighting under the standard of that greatest hope and inspiration of mankind, the United Nations, have liberated this ancient capital city of Korea... Its citizens once more have the opportunity to live under that immutable concept of life which holds invincibly to the primacy of individual liberty and personal dignity.'

— PRESS REPORT

Then Nobadaddy aloft
Farted and belched and coughed,
And said, 'I love hanging and drawing and quartering
Every bit as well as war and slaughtering.
Damn praying and singing,
Unless they will bring in
The blood of ten thousand by fighting or swinging.'

— WILLIAM BLAKE

Lamentation in Rama

Out of a sin
Scarcely original
A common pregnancy with all
The graceless discomforts
Of an upright animal –
Cherries her only craving
And a hard lying-in –

Blood and waters broke
Of metaphysical war:
Nor was her labour done
Until that parturition when
Caesarian surgery
Delivered from the swollen State
Her son slain by the law.

It had been better for us
If she had held her peace.
Only a trivial fuss
Exacerbates authority's
Impartial equilibrium:
A stirring in the womb
Alerts the testy police.

Surely she must have known
The gracious powers above
Keep watch on the little streets?
Someone was bound to inform.
The law was in need of delinquents,
The cross craved for meat.
The least suspicion of love –

Instant retaliation,
Trumpeters, taxes on salt,
Smoking settlements,
Folk dragged from their beds!
And what of the innocents?
Who was she to bring down
Herod about their heads?

Who will preserve the poor
From visitations of God,
From the law's solicitations
And the carnal lust of the drum?
Who will deliver them from
Evil consecutive upon
The contagion of the good?

Scenario for the Flight into Egypt

A misty still – the little town of Bethlehem.
Folk in the marketplace. A sexy woman,
Jar on her head. Dogs being dogs.
Then zoom in on Judaea. Motorway.
In leather gear, crash-helmeted,
Heaven's Angel wings it into town, doing a ton,
Slams on his anchors, hammers at Joseph's door...

Lucky to get a warning from the Lord!
He shakes his wife awake and tells her all is up.
She wraps her bastard in a rug, he gets his joiner's kit.
They flit it while the neighbours sleep.

Fade out. The nick of time. Dawn will pan
Enormous neuter platitudes of order
Crawling up every beach, full of marines.
Then track the fighter-bombers, serene technocrats,
Which shit their smoky excrement across the slums.
Space for development there. Blow up the bombs.
Blow up a woman's grieving face?
Blow up a bloody dog?
Enter artillery, to add up astronomical sums
Of injury, mixing the plaster with the blood.
And then the climax bit –
The rival holy armies, each in some other army's pay:
The prophets calling on their deaf and goofy gods –
Black streamers flapping in the sky, fire
Licking the minarets,
Snipers on the church roofs, grenades in the launderette.

We've got an epic there, vicarious as hell.
The viewers will identify. The rest is trite...
Let's see... Di da di da...
Bundles and broken carts. Roads machine-gunned.
Trucks overturned and burning.
Swarms of white-faced kids. Detritus of several cities –
The usual parts. Expensive, all those extras
Migrating through eternity like clichés!
Whatever's after them is always coming on:
Plague, famine, pogroms, taxes, wars, crusades...
The stubborn stamina of God's forgotten poor
Walking and walking down the centuries,
Trudging from someplace into nowhere-land.
Maybe a commentator vamps this bit
And makes the viewers yawn with pity?

What we shall need is human interest.
Let's bring back in those walk-on parts,
Lame Joseph with his staff, Mary in tears –
The bored centurions whistle at her back
With jokey brutish dancing, signifying rape.
Always the raging sun, always the lack of water.
Perhaps a close-up now...?

I see them resting at a turning in the road,
Where Joseph scoops a hollow in the sand,
And Mary gently lowers her heavy load.

Cut. Egypt. Zoom in on a squat.
Old Joseph planing at the bench. Mary at the tub.
The child – a toddler now – taking in all.
Heaven's Angel hammers at the door
And brings new marching-orders from the Lord.

All that way back only to fulfil
Some staring prophet's crackpot fantasies!
Poor fall-guy, scripted by some ancient hack,
Miscast as son of god by Judges 13.5 –
Old Joseph did his best to get him out of it –
Look, here's the text:
'And he arose and took the young child and his mother
And came into the land of Israel
But when he heard that Archelaus, son of Herod,
Did reign in Herod's place, and went on like his father,
He turned aside into the parts of Galilee,
And notwithstanding being warned of God
He brought the brat up as a carpenter...'

Boom, boom. Di da di da...
No mileage in the rest. The script gets messagey.
Heavy at times...Who would identify?
Cut to the final epic episode
Before the viewers switch the channel off...

'Enormous neuter platitudes of order
Crawl up the screens and occupy the news
Which musters at the place called Calvary.'

Prayer for the Year's Turning

*'I was looking on that Sign in the Heaven
which is called by the name of the Ballance.'*
SIR RICHARD STEELE

I

The cruel solstice of our kind,
The axletree of all is stuck –
There is no way of turning on
Nor any way of turning back.

Sign of the Balance, House of Mars,
Lord of the ascendant over Hope:
The stars in heaven look down on us
And shudder at earth's horoscope,

Where in our violent zodiac
New constellations exercise –
Trident is showing in the West,
Poseidon and Polaris rise

And Vulcan scuds across the moon.
Hades is setting over France
And, see, beside the Neutron Way,
The Fitter, Flogger and the Lance!

Oh kings and wizards, shield your eyes!
Oh shepherd, shepherdess, beware
Of following the Peacekeeper!
Oh loyal flock of sheep, take care
Lest the stars throw down their spears
And water heaven with our tears!

II

Oh watchers in the night, you watch
An emanation of yourselves,
And all that alien hardware is
Ourselves wheeling about ourselves.

Good people, do not watch the sky,
But keep your watchfulness below
And hasten with your gifts of love
To Newbury or Comiso,

And strike a match within the dark
To search about the planet's floor
For the nativity of hope
Like software stirring in the straw.

Oh fasten heaven back to earth
And stick in one the human race
And make the cargo of this globe
Less odious company in space!

Oh powers and influences, turn
Us into an ascendant House:
Oh fortune, budge your wheel once more!
Let this arrested solstice pass
Out of the boreal cold, and bring
The soft apocalypse of Spring...

[*Newbury or Comiso*: sites for Cruise missiles established in 1983]

POWERS AND NAMES

(1986)

(with apologies to Szuma Chien)

You have the power to name:
Naming gives power over all.
But who will name the power to name?
Asked the oracle.

Speech

Like a silkworm on a mulberry leaf
The unmannerly earth
Gnawed at the edge of the sky and bit out mountains.

Gorged with matter it dropped by the edge of the ocean,
Cocooned in unconsciousness and grass,
An existence unknown to itself,
Waiting to be spun by nimble tongues into languages.

Let us conciliate the powers by giving them names.
Let us swallow the worm.
Let us tame the world by taking it into ourselves.

Art

The dragons and the lions are furious.
They would like to eat us.
If we model their rage in clay
Will we drive terror away?

Naming the Gods

Ten suns flared in the sky.
They scorched the crops and hatched out of the clay
Fire-breathing demons. The great archer Yi
Chose from his pouch
Nine arrows flighted with a shaman's charm
And slew one sun with each, and ever after we
Named Yi as deity.

But Heaven's pillars cracked
And water gushed out of the broken arch,
Washing the corpses to the sea. So Nüwa raised
A paste of melted rocks
To patch the gashes in the sky, and from a giant turtle
She hewed its legs to prop Heaven back in place.
The goddess Nüwa be praised!

Then water must be educated
And led in levels to the fields. Yu the Great
Accomplished this in thirteen years of toil.
A winged dragon aided him
And once he changed himself into a bear
To scratch a passage through an obstinate hill.
We named Yu god of the soil

And Chi his son hereditary
Owner of all under Heaven, he and his family
In perpetuity. From that ancestral power
Sprouted the state:
Armies invented slavery: astronomy
Led the stars captive through the calendar:
Taxes invented the poor.

The Scholars

In scarcely a millennium
Spring diminished into autumn.
Was the world worse
In the time of incessant wars
Between the city states
Or were there benefits
For the autonomy of thought
In the competition of courts?

Congestion on the roads
As the scholars and their schools
Imagined luminous codes –
Ideologues and pedants,
An orator with an umbrella,
A sophist astride a mule,
A hermit in sandals of straw –
Pestered for audience,
Oppressed the courts of kings
And persecuted princes,
Urging them to restore
Obedience to Heaven's law.

When Confucius was lecturing
Lord Ling, the Duke of Vei,
Enforcing Heaven's rules
On the virtues of benevolence,
The Duke allowed his eyes
To leave his tutor and follow
Some wild geese in the sky.
At this indiscipline
Confucius took offence
And gathering up his school
Went off in a huff to Chen.

Says the Grand Historian:
It was a great mistake
To tutor power, for when
The law at last was learned
From legalist or mystic
By the Emperor of Chin
He ordered the imperial rule
Of benevolence to begin:
He buried the scholars alive
And the *Book of Songs* was burned.

O that Confucius
Had learned to keep his cool,
And had lingered to watch the geese
With the duke and his fool!

The First Emperor

In the 26th year of his reign the King of Chin
Assembled his counsellors.

In the desert of his nature little winds of boredom
Stirred eddies of dust. His throat was dry
And malice constricted his voice like that of a jackal.
Dust stirred in his slitted eyes. He said:
'I have conquered six states. I have captured or killed their kings.
Whoever opposed me has been enslaved.
All between the four seas has fallen under my rule.
I have defined the laws, making known what is forbidden,
And discovering (to the surprise of some) 600 degrees of sin
Hitherto nameless and now made manifest to all.
I have closed up the gaps in the Great Wall and garrisoned it
          from end to end.
What is there left for me to be omnipotent in?'

The counsellors bowed and puffed their sleeves:
The first minister, the marshall, the grand censor,
The executioner and the eunuchs of the royal commission.
They said: 'O thou ineffable Vocative!
Great Straightener, Almighty Regulator of All!
How couldst thou be more egregious than thou already art?
Thou hast brought letters level, made measures match,
And thou hast brought cash and morals into uniformity.
Men and women must now walk on different sides of the street,
Thanks to thy wisdom. Thou showest no favour no way.
Adulterers (if they are poor) may be boiled in cauldrons.
Officials abusing thy ordinances are always castrated.
Indeed, thy benevolence
Blesses the beasts in the fields, who press to the court,
Bleating to be thy meat. The water buffalo
Bellows thy name; the bees bring thee wax; the fish
Wish only to be thy dish; the rice crowds into the carts
And offers itself as tax…' Et cetera.

The King of Chin was gratified.
He ordered that their speeches be engraved upon stone
At the gateways to his 36 provinces.

Then he ascended a throne of alabaster
And, hiding his regal presence within veils,
Announced that Empire had commenced:

'Hereby I augurate a new age.
Lo, let us begin by renaming all names.
Since I have swallowed six kings I now assume plurality.
It is ordered that henceforth we shall be us,
Becoming Our First Exalted Sovereign Emperor.
Whatever we want will be known as Heaven's decree.
Our laws will be named edicts.
We hereby rename the poor our loyal black-headed people.
When we are satisfied all their wants are met,
When we eat the nation has been fed.
When we shit All have shat,
Oh, and since our brilliance will strike mortals blind,
Henceforth our imperial self will give audience only through screens
And we shall never be seen.'

The counsellors bowed and trembled for their balls.
They ordered to be engraved in stone on Mount Tai:
'The Sovereign Emperor made decrees and edicts which all his
        subjects heeded;
Great and manifest, his virtue is handed down to ages yet to
        come, to be followed without change.
The sage Emperor who has pacified all under Heaven is tireless in
        his rule;
He rises early and makes marginalia on his officials' reports;
He sets a standard of proper bearings and signs for all things;
The black-headed people are reformed; he surpasses the ancients
        and has never known error.
Oh gosh! he is so bright that he graciously saves our eyes by
        hiding behind screens.
His omnipotence knows no end, and his orders will be obeyed
        through eternity.'

The Emperor was pleased.
He sacrificed six white horses to the power of water,
Drowning them slowly. A picul of rice and a pig
Were ordered to be sent to every village in the land.
It was found (alas!) that demand exceeded supply,
But the intention (at least) was distributed to the poor,
Who raised their worn and empty hands
And blessed the Emperor.

Then he decreed that he had become immortal.
And was transmogrified. But was visited by doubt.
He sent boatloads of children out to find the fairy isles
Far in the misty eastern oceans where the immortals live.
They did not return. Perhaps they were stopped by whales?
He sent out alchemists to visit the barbarians,
In search of magic fungi and cunning elixirs.
But they were thwarted by demons...
Behind his screens the Emperor raged and aged.
He issued an edict condemning time:
'Whereas learning has confused our loyal BHP,
We abolish all histories which do not mention our name.

Let only despotic sciences be preserved:
Geometry, census, the computation of tax,
Econometrics, caryatics, castrametation, casuistics,
Cacodoxy, calculus, calibration, nefandous necromantics,
Decapitation, doctrinarianism and the division of parts.
Let the arts be banned,
And the *Book of Songs* be burned and the *Book of Music*.
Whoever recalls the past shall be cut in half
And whoever fails to report these crimes shall be burned with brands.'
The counsellors clapped their hands.

The Emperor retired into 200 palaces
Whose walls hung with the fungi of sycophancy.
The marsh creatures of lust clung around him.
He fed on sharks' fins and the pads of camels,
Tangerines, lychees and fantasies.
The white faces of treachery
Whispered around him and ministered to his lechery.

A eunuch hissed a signal of suspected treason,
The Emperor called in the scholars for a course of self-criticism.
They hastened to the court to incriminate each other.
Chuckling like a jackal he caused in the sands to be opened
A vault lit with dark lanterns
And stocked with the confiscated texts of Confucius.
460 sages were sent underground
To sound off in ghostly seminar through the ages.

Each day the Emperor rose and weighed his official reports.
He shifted half a picul of scrolls from his left to his right:
Ah, momentous inauguration of the dynasty of bumf!
According to auguries or according to the weather
He marked in the margins those he decreed to be dead.
On his capital errands
The palace eunuchs spurred with their imperial wands
In an incessant circulation of dread.

When he had first ascended to the throne of Chin
He had ordered work to begin on a bloody great tomb.
Now 700,000 castrati, convicts and slaves
Were impressed to Mount Li
To magnify his gigantic mausoleum
Which (however) the Emperor did not intend to go dead in,
Preferring to be an Eternal, whom water cannot wet,
Who rides on the clouds, impervious to fire,
And coeval with evil…

Changed name again. Became pure spirit.
We became It:
And, to fox the evil eye, It became invisible.
It flitted in secret
In screened arcades between Its 270 palaces.
Places of ecstasy, what with golden orioles
Shouting in the flowering cherries, and the lakes stocked
With exotic goldfish. Everywhere bells and drums
Exhorted the Eternal to come,
As did the countless beauties attendant on its every will
With which the pavilions and secret chambers were stacked.
Sheathed in green gauze
They back-combed their hair into pyramids like orchids
And languished for Its cock

(It having decreed that each must bear It a son
Or else...)
But were visited only by flaccid concupiscence
Since It could no longer fuck.

The Eternal flitted from palace to palace and moped.
It raged and aged.
It pawed and groped.
It wittered and moaned.
It decreed death
On any who disclosed where It was or where It might even be.
It issued an edict that It had ceased to exist
Except as despotic Essence.

You must imagine it now as pure vacancy

Here is Its Name:

              *   *   *

300 astrologers
Were abjured to conjure beneficent omens from the stars.
It ordered the spiritual purification of poetry:
The elimination of dentals, the utter ending of gutturals.
Musicians were ordered to oil their strings.
Ululation of sibilants and labials
As vowels howled in the shrouded corridors
And the pavilions wailed of immortality...

And in the 37th year of ascending to the throne of Chin
Eleven years on from assuming the name of We
And two years from the annunciation of spirituality
A stranger thrust into the censor's hand a disc of jade
On which was written The Primal Dragon Will Die!
And vanished in smoke...
                    In terror It fled.
It consulted oracles. It gave it out
That It had gone to inspect the empire's extremities.
For fear of lurking assassins
It sent forward convicts to fell the forests ahead.

114

Archers with crossbows marched in the vanguard
With orders to shoot all whales.
It remained invisible within a covered litter
Carried by slaves. It decreed the pains of hell
Upon any who mentioned death.
                                        And at Pingtai
In the 7th month of the 38th year
It died.
              But, being invisible, who could tell?

The first minister, Li Szu, thought the moment inauspicious.
He wasn't sure the old despot would stay dead.
Besides, he had designs on immortality himself,
By raising his creature, Hu-hai, to succeed as emperor
In place of the Crown Prince who had stayed in the capital.

Li Szu, Hu-hai, and the chosen eunuchs kept mum.

And so It continued on Its imperial progress
On the chariot roads in a swaying litter.
The BHP abased themselves before It.
The eunuchs humbly entered the screens bearing dishes
(Which they scoffed with relish within), ushering out
Flourishing fresh imperial decrees (drawn up by Li Szu).
Ah, then It was truly Idea
Disincarnate, aseptic apotheosis of Power,
Which issued an edict condemning Its own son and heir
(Who stood in the way of Hu-hai) and the Lord High Marshall
(Whom Li Szu disliked). Who both duly died
Of the death-sting of the invisible Eternal
Who at length began to stink to high heaven.
The stench caused gossip. To cover the matter
A cartload of salted fish was hitched to Its litter.

And in this manner the bizarre procession
Re-entered Hsienyang, capital of the empire,
Where the Prince and Marshall's heads grinned on the gates.
First came the outriders scouring for rice
Convicts with axes
Alchemists wishing for fungi
Augurers fishing for auguries
Archers warily watching for whales

The black imperial banners
Trumpeters, drummers
Then:
10,000 horsemen, 1000 charioteers
A myriad foot-soldiers sweating in full armour
Hu-hai, Li Szu, and the ministers of rank
The concubines swaying in palanquins
Eunuchs in rich insignia
Then:
The huge unfurled imperial dragon
The dead Eternal stinking in Its litter
And a cartload of salted fish.

A few explanations followed
Followed by exemplary executions.

After which It was borne
To the yawning mausoleum beneath Mount Li.
Laid in a coffin of copper
In a vault over which the constellations turned
And the floor was the world over which It had ruled
With the rivers and oceans sketched in mercury.
All the imperial palaces were modelled in jade:
Miraculous artifice guarded by gins and traps!
Oh, and those of the Eternal's ladies who had fallen down in
        their function
Of bearing It heirs (viz. male) (i.e. nearly all)
Were given the honour of going in gorgeous weeds
Into the vault to tend Its ghostly needs
And rub unguent on the offal.

In an afterthought
It was ordered to close the inner and outer gates
Upon the artificers and labourers
Who were also immured in that foetid space
So that they wouldn't betray the secrets of the place.

The Grand Historian erred
In neglecting to record where the fish were interred.

Rebellion

Suction of terror's swirling hysteria
Drew inwards all that could move on wheels or legs
In an acceleration of dread:
The livestock (including maidens).
Conscripts to close the tomb. Droves of geese.
Carts of millet. Pigs. What difference did
It make to be marked as dead

Or only as listed to die? 900 villagers
Were trudging west when the roads were barred by floods.
They were under orders to garrison the Wall,
Led by a farmer's son,
Chen Sheng who said: 'Since it has been decreed
That if we are late for duty the offence is capital,
What is the point of it all?'

Strange lights showed in the temples.
The foxes howled in prophecy:
'Heaven's mandate is withdrawn from Chin Shih Huang.'
A fisherman
Found in the belly of a carp a silken cloth
Marked in vermilion lettering:
'Chen Sheng will be the king.'

He killed the guards
And named himself as Magnifier of Chu.
The eastern provinces rose up against the west.
Villagers with their hoes
Cut down the governors, the collectors of tax,
And pillaged the palaces. In a ferocious harvest
They levelled and laid waste
All visible evidence of the Omnipotence
Who still lingered on as awe, an assertion of function
Unfulfilled, a need for Defence against the Huns.
It hissed in Its tomb
And advertised Its post as a vacancy
And from Its insatiate appetites began
The dynasty named as Han.

The Villagers

It had been the Emperor's whim
To have his armies buried with him,
But when the exchequer was destitute
He graciously stopped the soldiers' pay
And permitted them to substitute
Their persons precisely modelled in clay.

For an eternity the cows
Grazed round the tomb. No one could tell
Where under earth the warriors lay
Until in the time of immortal Mao
Labour brigaders sinking a well
Came on the mighty garrison
Still standing guard.
      As for the bones
Of the Emperor, the generations
Living beneath the ancestral mound
Have let two millennia pass:
It was best to leave It underground
And mow the last inch of grass.

The Warriors of Hsienyang

Clay-imaged warriors drilling in the sand
Stand ready to be inspected by war.
The kneeling archer has a lethal eye:
The deft fingers of the charioteer
Contain his mischievous horses as they shy.
The sergeant bullshits to belie his fear.
The browned-off soldiers waiting for commands
Are ready to fight but disinclined to die.

Rank upon rank their graven images
Stare through us into distant places.
We are their visions, like mirages
Which shimmer in the mirror of their faces.
Their scouts inspect us vacantly and say
That we are vapours plagiarising clay.

History Lessons

Neanderthal and Peking man
Barely survived the glacial age,
Neglecting to make a collective plan.

Accurate measurement of the brain
Reveals a capacity for speech.
This may be counted as a gain

And proves what Comrade Stalin said:
Tools manufactured humankind:
Necessity enlarged the head
And matter reflected itself as mind.

Art plays a contradictory role.
Scapulimancy was a trick
Used as a means of social control.

Magic's arcane languages
Cowed the masses within the caves
And established the shaman's privilege.

Astrologers served the ruling class
And sought in the stars a class reflection:
Society caught a religious infection
And primitive communism passed.

History marching through its phases
Found in the Emperor of Chin
A monarch to modernise its basis.

The superstructure united the nation
Determining a progressive mode
Of hydraulic civilisation.

However many the Emperor slew
The scientific historian
(While taking note of contradiction)
Affirms that productive forces grew.

The Rectification of Names

Heaven's mandate swarmed the land like locusts:
Taxation's inquisition racked the rocks and holes
Extracting the confession of their surplus.
The peasants hacked at famine with their hoes
And stirred the dirt to flower:
A hundred million hoes held up the vault of power.

Or was it propped up by the arch of awe
Whose proper name is self-expropriation?
If so, materialism turns a somersault:
We are the subjects of our own negation
And exploitation's basis floats
On the cold surface of our confiscated thought.

Modes of production like electric grids
Transmit us as their errands to their ends:
From matter's terminals to spirit's terminus
The circuits run as strict as continence,
Their only business to enforce
Relations of production into intercourse.

Necessity determinates our paths
Into preordinates in history's cassette:
We utter into print-out, ruled by roles,
And ranked like terracotta warriors. Yet
How could necessity dictate
That immane mausoleum, that predatory state,

Unless the programmer was high on mescalin?
Some manic ego in the mask of destiny
Dreams on the highest stair of ritual,
Hallucinating those despotic dynasties
Which know no longer what they are,
Forgetful of their origins in that exotic air.

Who tutored time in power's paradigms?
Did the Eternal on the stairs of Chin
Hallucinate our century's malignancies
And programme on our skies a swarm of acronyms?
It seems the aim of modern man
Is to fulfil the Emperor's two-millennial plan.

O starry Superalpha, terminal Amen!
Thou great First Cause, egregious Omega!
Our eunuchs and our censors clap their hands:
From day to day the unwearied media
Their great Original proclaim
And hallelujah their hosannahs to Thy Name.

O great totalitarian archetype
In whose ancestral influence we fall,
Who levelled all to uniformity and left
Humanity bisected by a Wall:
Know that all progress tends
To modernise Thy Means and end Thy Awful Ends.

The whale-oil gutters in the lamps below.
The vault is sealed. The women fear to stir
Their shadows which are threatening themselves.
Each sings and suffers with her sisters,
Ending as she began
In awe and incense and the categories of man.

Abstraction dreams of destiny again.
The mind is sealed with absolute nouns
Which steal our names and alienate our powers:
The Emperor hisses in his funeral mound.
It's time the oppressed arose
And cut down categories with their hoes.

From the green earth's imagined holocaust
Arise ye starveling images and blow
Our servile minds out of their algorithms
And blow the fuse of history's teleo:
Arise and repossess
The surplus value of your swindled consciousness!

Plato thought nature plagiarises spirit:
Being determines consciousness determined Marx:
But in the contradictions of the Way
The human dialectic osculates and arcs
And quarrels to insert
Some transient motive in the motiveless inert.

By getting right the proper names of things
Confucius said that order would commence,
And Taoism taught all would be kind
If they forgot about 'benevolence':
Cut down the props, the skies above
Will still hold up upon the menial rites of love

Whose needs are the material habitus
From which the goddesses and dragons came,
Whose archers will shoot down the nuclear fire,
Whose nameless pillars are imagination's flames,
Whose arcane oracles proclaim
The rectification of the human name.

A Charm Against Evil

Throw the forbidden places open.
Let the dragons and the lions play.
Let us swallow the worm of power
And the name pass away.

Fred Inglis was a junior officer in the Parachute Regiment during his National Service, before reading English Literature at Cambridge. He is now Professor of Cultural Studies at the University of Sheffield. He was Chair of CND in the South West from 1979 to 1985, and for some years Secretary of END. He was four times a parliamentary candidate for the Labour Party between 1970 and 1987. He has been a member of the School of Social Science at the Institute for Advanced Study, Princeton, and was Fellow in Residence at the Netherlands Institute for Advanced Study in the Humanities and Social Sciences in 1998-99.

His books include *The Cruel Peace: Everyday Life and the Cold War* (Basic Books, 1992), in which the Thompson brothers feature prominently, *Raymond Williams: The Life* (Routledge, 1995), and *The Journalist in Modern Politics* (Yale University Press, forthcoming).